THINK LIK
ACT LIKE A PRO

"Al's ability to translate the principles he learned as an All Pro Athlete to a game plan for life and business is unmatched. A great teammate and leader."

— Eddie George,
1996 Heisman Trophy Winner and All Pro Running Back

"After knowing Al Smith for many years, I can say the title of his book *Think like a Pro, Act like a Pro* says it all! It is a testament to the values that he has exemplified on the field and off the field. He has embodied the impeccable qualities of great inspiration, courage, and hope. In his book, every word rings with truth as he lays out his steps to developing the human spirit."

— Senator Thelma Harper,
State of Tennessee

"As a speaker, Al Smith has been an insightful, inspirational leader to our doctors all over the world. As an author, Al has done a fantastic job in writing a book that reveals the kind of mindset, character, and work ethic it takes to be in that top 1/10th of 1% not just in the NFL, but in any field of endeavor."

— Dr. Ben Lerner,
Two time NY Times Best Selling Author and Co-founder of
Maximized Living Health Centers

"Al Smith spells out seventeen relevant and timeless strategies for all facets of life. Those who choose to follow this guidance will be rewarded."

— John Ingram,
Chairman and CEO of the Ingram Group

"Al has a unique four angle perspective that very few have: NFL All Pro linebacker, NFL front office executive, husband and dad. These four angles give him immense resources to pull from in developing his seventeen life strategies for success."

— Jerry Reese,
Senior Vice President and General Manager New York Football Giants and winner of Super Bowls XLII & XLVI

"You don't have to be an NFL fan to enjoy *Think Like A Pro, Act Like A Pro*. This book transcends the sports and corporate worlds; you will come away entertained and inspired by Smith's revealing look inside the All Pro mindset of a former NFL star."

— John McClain,
NFL Writer for the Houston Chronicle (37 years)

"This is a great book, a moving account of a difficult passage, full of heart and wisdom. It is an offering from a true spiritual friend. Think like a Pro, Act like a Pro is sure to serve as a support and inspiration for many."

— Kanye Harris,
Delta Airlines Executive Global Distributions

"Al walks the talk and can be counted on to deliver. I have watched Al become a great business man and community leader in Nashville and middle Tennessee. A man of few words but many talents, positive actions and successful results. The principles within *Think Like A Pro, Act Like A Pro*' are life changing and inspirational."

— Carl T. Haley, JR
President & CEO, Grand Avenue

"Al is a dynamic speaker with exceptional leadership success both on and off the field. He possesses over 25 years of experience from NFL player to Front Office Executive, his business strategies both deliver and inspire."

— Ron Jaworski, ESPN Analyst

"In my work as a licensed mental health counselor and business leader, I have opportunity to meet with many people facing various challenges in life. Al Smith is clear about the importance of character in our lives and our relationships—character counts. Through his life he inspires others to remember that character is our responsibility to build through the choices we make and the principles we live by. This book shares truth in a unique and compelling way."

— Rich Blue,
Founder and Clinical Director for Center for Christian Life Enrichment; Speaker, Author of *"Surprised By God"*

"In life and in business I've learned its best to surround yourself with people who exhibit strong moral character. Most everything else can be trained. Al Smith has provided an outstanding playbook for any person who wants to achieve their dreams while living a life of purpose and with integrity."

— Kris DenBesten,
President, Vermeer Southeast, Author, Speaker

THINK LIKE A PRO - ACT LIKE A PRO

Game-winning Strategies to Achieve Results, Discipline, and Success in Life and Business

AL SMITH

FORMER NFL ALL-PRO LINEBACKER

HIGHERLIFE
PUBLISHING & MARKETING
www.ahigherlife.com

Think Like A Pro — Act Like A Pro by Al Smith
Published by
HigherLife Publishing & Marketing, Inc.
PO Box 623307
Oviedo, Florida 32762
www.ahigherlife.com

Scripture quotations, unless otherwise noted, are from the English Standard Version of the Bible. Used by permission.

Interior Design: Dimitreus Castro
Cover Design: Dimitreus Castro

ISBN: 978-1-939183-77-4
Library of Congress Cataloging in Publication Data

Printed in the United States of America

"Success is never final and failure is never fatal. It's courage that counts."

— Sir Winston Churchill

DEDICATION

This book is dedicated to my amazing mother, Eunice Smith, who always said that the two most important days of my life were the day I was born and the day I discovered why I was born. Thank you, Mom, for all you did for me and our family! I have found my purpose.

To my father, AC Smith, who helped make me who I am today and for showing me what hard work is.

To my oldest brother, Aaron, who was a gifted student and athlete. Thank you for showing me the right path to take and always having my back. I can't wait till we are together once again.

To my son, Christian, for all that you are and will become! May you grow to be a better man than me, have bigger dreams than mine and the capability to make those dreams come true!

Thank you to all the great teammates who taught me so much, including Warren Moon, Bruce Matthews, Mike Munchak, Spencer Tillman and Lee Williams, all great leaders.

To my wife, Katrina. whom I met toward the end of my career with the NFL, your impact on my life and those around us is immeasurable. I love you for all your love and support.

To my daughters, Courtney and Coryn. It is my hope that you will grow up and change the world. You add something special to my life, and I am grateful for each moment I share with each of you.

To my two sisters, Vickie and Demetra, who were there all along in my journey, I couldn't ask for better sisters. Thank you for your support and encouragement every step of the way.

THINK LIKE A PRO - ACT LIKE A PRO

Game-winning Strategies to Achieve Results, Discipline, and Success in Life and Business

ABOUT THE AUTHOR

Al Smith is a former National Football League player, an executive, author, and speaker with over 25 years of leadership experience. He learned discipline, structure, and values from his mother. Al continues to help people strive toward and achieve their goals. A former executive with the Tennessee Titans, NFL Alumni President and Sports Analyst, and former Director of Player Development at Vanderbilt University in Nashville, Tennessee and serves on the Board of Directors for the NFL Alumni Association and the American Cancer Society. Al has contributed to multiple organizations including Big Brothers Big Sisters, Bridges Domestic Violence Center and the Ronald McDonald House. Al is also an Ambassador with Fuel Up to Play 60.

Al grew up loving the game of football and was offered multiple scholarships to play on the collegiate level. He chose to attend college in Utah and play for the Utah State Aggies. A standout collegiate player and team leader, Al was inducted into the Utah State Athletic Hall of Fame and selected for the state of Utah All-Century team. In 1987, he was drafted by the Houston Oilers and became an immediate starter for the team as a rookie. The Oilers finished 9-6 that year and were second in their division.

Al played with the Oilers from 1987 to 1996. His teammates in-cluded NFL legends such as all-time franchise passing leader Warren Moon, all-time team rushing leader and Heisman Trophy winner

Eddie George, Pro Football Hall of Fame inductee Bruce Matthews, quarterback Steve McNair, Heisman Trophy winner Mike Rozler, team receiving leader Ernest Givins, and nine time All-Pro and NFL Hall of Famer Mike Munchak. He was coached by Jeff Fisher, the franchise's all-time winningest coach. Al's career in the NFL included two Pro Bowl selections, multiple first alternate honors and first-team All-Pro honors.

INTRODUCTION

This isn't a book about sports. It's a book about character, leadership, adversity, and strength. Each one of us can think like a pro on and off the field. It doesn't matter what your job, career or family situation look like. Now is the time to think like a pro and sharpen your skills.

Why do some people seem to just get it and rise above everyone else? These people do not go through life without challenges, but they are well prepared for whatever life puts in their way.

Certainly they leverage their God-given talents and physical abilities. But even those who have speed or great hand-eye coordination still have to be able to channel it the proper way and manage the curves and bumps encountered along life's road. How many times have you read the newspaper or watched the television news and saw someone who was thrown one of life's curve balls? Their legacy and destiny are altered forever.

We have all read the story of the collegiate star athlete who could not make it to the next level and was grounded just before he took off. Many times the demands of the endeavor uncovered personality weaknesses and deficiencies in preparation so that something the person in question badly needed was not available at the right moment. The lessons within this book are like layers of paint that build on top of one another—base coat, color, and glaze—to finally provide a strong and consistent protection. The goal is that these lessons will provide those components necessary to reach the next level when the time comes.

The first question to consider: How strong are the mentors in your life?

I had a phenomenal football career, but I also had a series of mentors in my life. Some of my life's lessons were hard and some easier, but they all served to help me along my path. I had my share of setbacks, struggles, and tests, but through it all, I was fortunate to have everyone God put into my life. If I could line everyone up to thank them personally, the line would start and end with my mother.

One of the greatest influences in my life, my mother, Eunice, said the two most important days in my life were the day I was born and the day I figured out why I was born. She was instrumental in encouraging me and led me down the path to finding my purpose. She passed away in the summer of 2014 after battling cancer.

I write in the hope that I can honor my mother's memory and the role she played in my life. She instilled good habits in me at a very early age. My focus on walking with integrity, and ultimately being professional, all stemmed from her training. She taught me about speaking and how our actions transcend our words. Even as a child, I appreciated her wisdom. Communication with friends, teachers, and coaches was easier with her guidance. When I was in uncomfortable situations, I relied on her experience and her example.

Others have taken up her mantle, but it was her influence that propelled me through high school, through college, and into my professional life.

I also loved and respected my dad. He was a hardworking, disciplined man—a no-nonsense person who did not sugarcoat things. He got straight to the point. I had many mentors growing up, but these two were most important; they raised me.

Whether you have mentors or not, you can continually make a commitment to step up. Rise up and learn. Be a mentor yourself, but also have one.

We have all witnessed people who have tried to take shortcuts, ignored those who have tried to help them, or missed a critical lesson or two along the way. How many of us have had a conversation or two with a lost high school athlete who just couldn't maximize the potential he or she had and ended up stranded in a small town with little opportunity? All of those "wannabes" had their hopes cut short—not because of physical issues, but because of a missing lesson or teaching. Some lessons are truly needed in life; if they are missed, progress is inhibited, even stopped.

It's like having a leaky container. No matter what you do or how fast you travel with the full bucket, you will always lose water. Eventually, more cracks and damage can occur, rendering the bucket useless. But if the hole in the bucket is repaired, it can function well, almost like new.

When you look closely at those who move forward in a positive manner and analyze their past, a few points can be made:

1. They surrounded themselves with a small number of people who were constantly connected with them in most phases of their lives. These people became sounding boards, advisors who helped them smooth out any bumps or challenges along the way.
2. They learned fast and usually did not make the same mistake twice.
3. They possessed all or almost all of the character traits outlined in this book.

I was fortunate in life because I had a good foundation and role models who showed me the way. I really didn't know it at the time. God provided mentors to step into my life in the form of a sister, brother, teacher, or friend; each of them provided something I needed. It was always the right person at the right time.

To be successful in life, it is very important to have a mentor, a coach, someone with more experience than you, someone who is in a position in life that you desire to reach in the future or someone you trust who can help you fulfill your calling.

Most people underestimate the value of a mentor. This is the biggest reason for failure in business and life in general. Everyone needs a mentor. Everyone needs someone they can go to and lean on, someone they know is in their corner. It's like having a success coach who makes sure you get the resources, feedback, and insights that will help you reach your full potential. Whether you have a mentor or not, you can continually make a commitment to step up. Rise up and learn. Be a mentor yourself, but also have one.

It's unusual for people to learn every lesson the same way. All our life lessons are part of a big puzzle. Each piece has a place in a larger image. Some pieces may be more important than others, but without all the pieces—and even though you may be able to guess what the image is—something will always be missing.

I wrote this book to give readers a few important tools for success. The lessons I will relate are ones I learned on and off the field. Some were intentional and others I learned the hard way. I learned about discipline, hard work, and sacrifice. I learned that during times of adversity and uncertainty and struggle, you can actually stay focused, and come out on the other end a better person.

LIFE STRATEGIES FOR SUCCESS

"CHARACTER"

Character is invisible, but we see it every day in one's actions and words. Abraham Lincoln wrote, "Reputation is the shadow. Character is the tree." A person's character consists of much more than what we want others to see; it is who we are, even when no one is watching.

Character is the essence of a person. At the core of a person's being, there are beliefs and attitudes that drive one's actions. This dynamic is the basis of one's character. Character gets tested every day in every situation where you are asked to make a decision. Character is made up of

> **Good character is choosing to do the right thing because it is the right thing to do, no matter what.**

the delicate mix and balance of your life experiences, the values you have gained, been taught, or observed, and the definition and pursuit

1

of one's life vision. Of course, all of these are measured against their overall acceptance in today's society. Your character shows who you actually are.

Your character will set the stage for what determines your success in any area of life. Character guides our responses to all situations or circumstances in our life. It is why we do the things we do, and it is why we do things the way we do them.

In business as well as in sports, there are people who have special and unique talents that attract you to them. You want to be like them. You see how they handle themselves in a meeting; you see how they interact and handle situations. You might want to emulate the personality or character of someone special like this. The fact is that you are also special. It's important that you become the person you are called to be.

Building character is a lifelong process. Most people are in the middle of that process and are not yet all that they are meant to be. This is normal. Sometimes your environment is not conducive to positive growth and the people around you have bad character. Your responses to situations will determine the results you get. The bottom line is that your success in any endeavor will be determined by your character. This is one of the reasons you should not try to be someone you are not. You cannot be what you are not, just as you cannot give what you do not have. All behaviors are communication. When someone acts "out of character," they are trying to tell us something is wrong.

When I played football, there were talented guys with good character, and talented guys with not-so-good character. The ones with good character are the ones I remember most because of their positive actions or words. You remember people who positively impact your life. You remember the great things they did for you.

I grew up in the City of Angels, Los Angeles, California: a myriad of cultures in a large city. This diverse population provided many influences—the good, the bad and the ugly. I had many choices to make. Oddly enough, I found that to be to my advantage. Growing up there, I was exposed to many different lifestyles, cultures, and philosophies.

Although this had the potential to promote the development of unhealthy habits, I was fortunate to be in a family circle that possessed great values. My older brother, Aaron, was a standout athlete and student who reinforced these values—not just athletically, but academically. He really showed me the essence of what it meant to be a student athlete, with the emphasis on student.

Aaron has passed away, but in his short life he provided great mentorship and motivation for me. We grew up in the same home, in the same room. I was driven and encouraged to raise my standards by his performance and achievements, and because of that, I was inspired to reach his model of excellence. Instead of being in competition with my brother as many kids are, I looked up to him, and wanted to be like him. He paved the way for me, setting the bar for me to meet his expectations, both academically and athletically. He was both a great student and a great athlete. Aaron received a college scholarship to play ball and went on to play professionally.

Character comes down to you and your choices. The best of mentors cannot force you to make the right decisions or form good character in you. Along the way, I had choices to make. There were many opportunities to not follow in my brother's footsteps, but each time I was tempted to go in a different direction, I held fast. I could have strayed from the plan, or embraced the challenge and follow the course. I ended up staying the course. We all have similar choices to make.

There were times when I was faced with the temptation to go down the wrong path and find negative rewards, but fortunately, I had a circle of supporters who cared enough about me to point out where I was headed. Have you ever had angels like that come along when you were just about to make a very bad decision? Those who helped me had witnessed others on the same path; they had seen the destructive results of unhealthy and self-centered choices. These mentors in my life reminded me of my responsibility to my family and urged me to take the better road. I did not want to tarnish our family name. If I ever started to forget that, they were there to remind me.

What about you? Have you given thought to the kind of character you have had until this point in your life?

Having a mentor or coach can help you decipher your challenges and actions, help you better understand what you are facing, and help you anticipate the impact of your decisions. A mentor doesn't direct your life; he or she comes alongside you as you encounter life's issues.

> **Your character drives how you live; it's seen every time you speak, and shown in the way you react in times of struggle.**

Things change rapidly. Today, the requirements for success in business may be one way, and tomorrow they could be very different. Life's success will take on new meanings in the global information exchange. Successful people will need to be more and more flexible and diverse; they will have to provide solutions to clients anywhere in the world, anytime, day or night. The time when you could take a few days to carefully craft a well considered response to a letter you received is long gone. In today's instant gratification environment, people expect to receive a reply not in the mail, and maybe not even by e-mail, but by an immediate text reply.

Just as things change, so will some of the qualities and traits for long-term success change. Are you developing the right plan to achieve your goals? Are your goals achievable? Are they big enough?

My high school principal also greatly influenced my life. He was a retired army colonel who instilled discipline in my life. Colonel Hughes was a larger-than-life, imposing figure. I graduated from St. Bernard Catholic High School in Playa Del Rey, California. The colonel's presence was not easily missed. He was 6 feet, 5 inches tall, bald, and ran a mighty tight ship. His idea of maintaining order, accountability, and discipline made quite an impression on me. He placed great emphasis on our grades. It did not matter which sport we played; if we expected to play, he insisted we had satisfactory grades. He did not waver. His role as a disciplinarian made a great impact on my life. I greatly value my experiences and the lessons those experiences taught me. In my playing days, I was always a starter, never a backup. I never sat on the bench and watched the others play. I had to work with my team to achieve our purpose. Being prepared, trusting others and communicating effectively as part of a team build a foundation for working together. Each individual has a unique vision when presented with an opportunity, but by respectfully sharing ideas and being accountable to the team, great goals can be realized by everyone.

Humility, respect for others, accountability, and perseverance are all valuable character traits. While displaying courage and self-confidence in a leadership role or as a member of the team, it is imperative not to lose the lesson in the process—especially when you lose. You have the capability to change your circumstances, no matter who you are with: friends, teachers, coaches, or colleagues, and even when you feel stuck or are in a seemingly hopeless situation.

> **You have a responsibility not just to others, but to yourself. We all do.**

This is my message and what I was taught as a child. We aren't here just to take up space. How will you behave, serve, observe, and respond? This book will help you develop your skills and think about the way you're responding to others.

People behave differently depending on their audience. How do you behave in the company of authority figures, when someone is watching? Your true character is evident in the way you behave when you don't think anyone is watching.

Above all, it is imperative that we respect our family name. Our personal brand. If I got into any trouble, I knew it would not only harm my reputation, but also the name of my team. My brand. I represent my family, my team, my organization every day, with every decision I make. We have the responsibility to consider our parents, siblings, and team members when we make decisions. It is my hope that I will leave a legacy for my son and daughter. I believe that by making it a point to always choose to do the right thing, respecting God as someone greater than myself, and believing that I am not the center of this family, but He is, I will leave a healthy legacy and make a great impact on my children.

Character counts. That's not just some saying in a book. It's true! I hope to inspire you to think about the important things in your life. It's not just my football career that matters. That's only part of my legacy. It's not about being perfect. It's about living my life the best possible way. There are no shortcuts. The important thing is how many people I can impact, and choosing to have good character. There are no shortcuts.

Identify and focus on the things that are important to you. I have chosen to intentionally pass on particular values, beliefs, and traits to my family because I think they are important. I think they matter because my experience has taught me that they do.

What does your character say about you?

What will you be remembered for?

STEPS TO BUILD CHARACTER

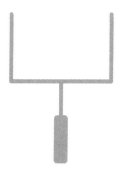

Grab a notebook and make a list of the five specific character traits you want to be known for. Maybe loyalty, humility, honor, punctuality, love, or discipline come to mind. Maybe it's being reliable. Only you know what you value most. Talk to your mentor about your list. Ask him or her if there is anything else they think should be on it. Allow your mentor to speak into your life.

Additionally, ask your mentor to give you direction about ways to build these character traits you have discussed.

Above all, make the right choices. Choose character over everything else, such as money or skill or temptation.

To build character, surround yourself with people who have good character.

"Focus"

What does it mean to focus?

No matter who you are, you've got to have focus in order to succeed in life. It doesn't matter if you're a teacher, executive, stay-at-home parent, plumber, athlete, or student.

To focus means that you are setting your sights on *one thing*, to concentrate, and to be fully committed. Sports teach you how to focus. In order to be successful in the position you are playing, ability and focus have to meet. It's the same way in life.

Focus is necessary to execute any task! How strong are you in your ability to focus?

If we are focused, we are concentrated on a goal; we have direction. We have an idea of what we want to be or where we want to go in life.

Being an athlete teaches you to be persistent in your focus, but this trait is necessary to successfully develop in any vocation. We all need to persevere through mistakes, failure, and adversity, to remain focused even when the situation and the outcome seems unfavorable.

Any CEO or professional athlete can tell you that being able to focus contributed to his or her success. No matter what kind of job you have, your dedication and commitment is necessary. Will you give it your all? Or will you do things halfway?

Take a moment and consider the people you have seen who didn't do the things they should have done because they didn't live up to their potential or because they allowed distractions to steal their focus. Don't be that guy. Don't be the one who takes the shortcut. Be focused. Be diligent.

When I played football, I learned a lot about how to stay focused even under the harshest conditions. Playing a sport can prepare you for these moments. There were times when we were being outplayed and times when we were outmatched, but by remaining focused on the game, we were able to capitalize on turnovers or make plays that changed the course of the game.

It's the same way with life. You can go through a difficult situation in life, but if you remain focused, you can bounce back and overcome any obstacle. In fact, difficult situations can actually make you stronger.

What are you focusing on?

If you're having trouble figuring it out, get a mentor. You'll hear me talking about this throughout the book, and it applies to every lesson we cover. Mentors are simply humans who have already reached the level for which you're striving. They can help you get focused on your goals and dreams.

A mentor will help you prevent mistakes that you otherwise would have no way of avoiding. There are only two ways to gain wisdom in life: making your own mistakes or learning from others' mistakes. Your friends will tolerate your weaknesses and shortcomings, but your mentor will work to identify those weaknesses and shortcomings and invest time in you to help you remove them entirely.

Your friends have knowledge of your past, but your mentor is more focused on your future. A good mentor will stretch you just by being in your presence because they know and understand you better than you understand yourself.

Remember that all professional athletes—no matter how great they are—have a coach. It takes a certain type of person to bring out undeveloped talents and abilities in people. Talent cannot be taught. This is why coaches are more valuable than players. Without good coaches, talent would stay hidden. A good mentor will help bring out the best in you when you don't necessarily see the qualities you possess.

When you lack focus or need to be reminded what your focus should be, your mentor can help you get back where you belong, and point you in the right direction again.

One of the hallmarks of a good mentor is that he or she will always tell you the truth. Your mentor's primary objective is to make sure you are successful. Your friends and family might tell you what you want to hear, but a mentor will tell you what you *need* to hear. This is not always easy to do because of ego issues, especially in men. There were times I did not want to hear correction! But a good mentor understands that a day of tension is better than a lifetime of regret, and as a result will always tell you the truth. Mentors are invested in your success, so they will never let you believe you have arrived at your destination when you really haven't. They will faithfully help you stay focused and going in the right direction.

> **But a good mentor understands that a day of tension is better than a lifetime of regret, and as a result will always tell you the truth.**

STEPS TO GET FOCUSED

If you don't have a mentor, get one. Ask the mentor to help you focus.

Direct your energy toward your passion. Once you do that, life will be less confusing.

In your notebook, jot down some of your lifetime goals. Go over the list with your mentor. Are you on the right track to meet those goals? Are you focused on the best pursuits?

Eliminate distractions. This is the very best way to achieve your goals. Don't let distractions pull you away from your dream.

"Teamwork"

Everyone knows the value of teamwork, yet it can be hard to live it. One of the best sayings ever written is that, "teamwork makes the dream work." It's catchy and it's true! Ask any successful businessman, parent, sports official, player, or member of any family about the concept of teamwork.

He or she will tell you that teamwork played a big part in their success. Having a group of people achieve a common goal makes the road to success a lot easier to travel. But not everyone was raised to be a team player. Were you? I learned the value in working as a team at home and in sports. Not everyone understands this concept or how valuable it is when applied to life. Teamwork is a crucial element for the success of a marriage or a corporate board.

What does it mean to work as a team? Anyone can have teammates, but where there's teamwork, a lot more is possible. Teamwork means that everyone has each other's best interest at heart, and success hinges on the common goal of the team.

13

Howard Schultz, the owner of Starbucks, created a great company built on teams. He said that to be successful, he had to give up ownership, meaning he had to delegate duties and trust in the abilities of other people. He saw the value of teamwork. Understanding this concept will increase our chances of being successful. It takes a good team to be successful. No matter the undertaking, having a group you can depend on is essential for success.

By playing sports, I learned that a team does not exist because of individual teammates. A team exists because of *teamwork*. When building a team, you want to be careful not to attract people who simply don't understand the concept of teamwork. Teamwork requires you to be supportive of the whole group as well as expect their support. Playing sports taught me that you can achieve more with teamwork than you can achieve alone. Teamwork motivates you to do your best. Everyone succeeds when the goal is met.

What does teamwork mean to you?

When I think of it now, my understanding hasn't changed at all, even though I no longer play professional sports. Teamwork is a critical part of life—one that matters in every family, every friendship, every partnership. Even if you're taking a vacation, teamwork comes into play because everyone has a different idea of where he or she wants to go and wants to do when they get there. Actually, you have to work as a team when it's time to decide at which restaurant you choose to eat as a family. You can't steamroll over everyone else's opinion, because if you do, they won't invite you out with them next time!

> **Teamwork is a critical part of life—one that matters in every family, every friendship, every partnership.**

Everyone is part of a team whether they want to be or not. The question is, are you a good team member? A good team member is considerate of others' needs. One of the character traits of a leader is the ability to be giving, considerate, and deliberate.

As an athlete, family member, or participant in any relationship or business endeavor, you have the opportunity to be part of a team. Teams are not just individuals who belong to certain groups or organizations. Teams involve cooperation; each person must work together as one unit to achieve a common goal. This might seem obvious, but we must not forget it. Take it as a gentle reminder to assess and evaluate your own leadership and teamwork skills.

If you've never played a sport, it may be difficult to fully understand the importance of teamwork and why it is essential in every aspect of life. To have success, you have to direct your attitude toward group potential and opportunity. As an athlete, it's critical to be dedicated to the good of the team as a whole. No matter what team you're part of, it's likely that the group is composed of a variety of individuals coming from different backgrounds, different states, and different cultures. You're placed in a unique position—a position that gives you an opportunity to understand the blueprint for success. You're taught that you will have to believe, trust, and rely on others to be successful. This is an attitude you should have if you want to be successful in life.

What does teamwork mean to you?

The way you get the lesson delivered in sports is when you realize that for you to have success as an individual, the team has to be successful as well. I've been married awhile now, and I can tell you it's the same way in relationships. You want the whole team to win, not just one member of it.

The concept of working as one unit or one force must be instilled in your mental outlook. Being part of a team gives you the opportunity to develop your people skills. On a team, you are forced to communicate—whether it is through calling plays, giving advice, or setting the direction. Being able to communicate plays a major role in the success of that team. It also develops the character needed for leadership.

A team bands together when there's a mission greater than the team members themselves.

In football, there was also the understanding that it was rare for a scout to travel to see an all-star player on a losing team. So the success of the team is important for the success of its individual players as well. I'm not saying that you have to like all your teammates. I didn't, but I respected them in that we all worked for the best interest of the group. I had regard for that—that when the team was successful, everyone achieved. Not only do the most valuable players shine, but the team is in the spotlight as well.

Coaches understand this. When you participate in a sport, you gain this understanding as well. You're in a valuable position to learn the keys to success in life. It takes communicating and the establishment of relationships with other human beings to experience any amount of real success in life.

THE POWER OF MULTIPLICATION

Think of how powerful more than one person can be in communicating a message. Whether it's in social media or anywhere else, the power of communication isn't in one voice, but many. Movements have been created by many, many voices standing together. It takes teamwork to get a bill passed in Congress; many people working together abolished slavery; teamwork is involved in putting out an amazing new proposal within an organization. How about the teamwork involved in presenting to, and landing, a new client?

The pathways to success revolve around the relationships we establish with other people. No one said those relationships have to be perfect, but they must at least be accommodating in that they support you and your efforts toward success in life.

If your results are suffering at home, in a relationship, or inside an organization, shift your focus and efforts on teamwork. Instead of pushing harder, try to evaluate areas in which you can build the cohesiveness or morale of the group. Every individual team member is a player and contributor who will help push the ball down the field. The individuals can work together to progress and have success through the power of multiplication.

Check your team, and work on nurturing it in order to achieve greater results.

This is a solution for leaders. If you're not achieving the sales numbers, cohesiveness or results you need, in what way can you effectively integrate leadership into the individuals on your team? Individuals won't fight for nothing at all. Individuals only bond and come together as a team if they're fighting for something that matters. You absolutely must give them a purpose. If you're a leader, the purpose has to be far greater than the hope of a promotion or a sale. It has to be a strong link to their beliefs that they're making a difference, achieving more and impacting lives. What do you stand for? What's your mission?

Think of it in the way a football team or an army on the field fights the opposition. Warriors band together. They fight for a common goal. They believe in a common purpose, and it goes much deeper than their paycheck and the individual rewards. Great leaders understand that movements and winning are linked first to core values.

STEPS FOR STRENGTHENING TEAMS

Think about your contribution. Do your job. Give more. How can you be a better team member? Sometimes, the best answers are simple. Do what you are required to do when you're required to do it.

Actively think about the ways you help team members and the ways they help you. This may be an area in which you can grow even more. (It is for most people.) Talk with your leader about being a better part of your team.

Your team isn't found just on the field or in the workplace; it is also at home.

What does your family stand for? What are your core values? Review them and come up with a plan to achieve your goals. Remember: teamwork makes the dream work.

"Teamwork makes the dream work...."

-John C. Maxwell, author

STRATEGY 4

"DISCIPLINE"

f you looked at your life, in what areas would you say you need to be more disciplined? Discipline is the foundation for productive behavior patterns and the fuel for success in life. It is a fundamental fact that where there's no discipline, there's an excuse for failure.

Think about that for a moment.

If you lack discipline, you're going to fail at losing weight, stopping smoking, writing that proposal, becoming an excellent speaker, or anything else you want to do. If you don't teach your kids discipline, it's possible they won't be tough enough to endure, follow rules, or get up early to work out or study. Discipline is the key to achieving anything in life. It's the antidote to laziness.

Coaches use different methods for teaching discipline, but they all understand that through discipline comes desire, the heart and soul of the sport.

The moment you enter that locker room for the first time, coaches are either already aware of your abilities or about to discover them. Most coaches are more concerned with whether or not you are disciplined, or can be taught discipline. If you have discipline, you can learn to work with others.

Discipline starts somewhere. My parents taught us discipline. But some parents do not, and as a result, you find adults without any concept of how to create strong habits or discipline in their lives. Without discipline, it is impossible to save money, lose weight, build a business, or strengthen your body or mind.

Discipline should be introduced early in life, so we understand its value. Otherwise, we can be disciplined in some areas and need to develop discipline in others. It's never too late to make a commitment to be disciplined in your own life. Want to lose ten pounds? You get what you focus on. Get up and work out for an hour every day, and it'll happen. Want to start a business? Get disciplined about carving out time to make it happen. When I decided to write a book, I had nothing but ideas. I wanted to do well, so I decided to hire a writing coach who would help me organize my ideas and encourage me along the way. I knew that I needed that to stay disciplined!

Hard work and discipline lead to strength and perseverance that cannot be replaced.

How about you? In what areas do you need to invest in yourself, or a coach, to stay disciplined enough to fulfill your dream? The key is to get the discipline you need—whether you've got to manufacture it by getting a mentor or coach who can inspire and push you and hold you accountable, or whether you've got it burning inside already. Discipline comes easier when you've got a mission that's greater than yourself. It's easier to stay disciplined when you're focused on a project that can change lives; discipline is important and becomes the fuel to get you there.

I was blessed to learn how to become disciplined. My parents were very focused on education as a source of achievement in our lives. School was the one thing you were not going to miss. You had to be practically dying to get out of going to school. And if I wasn't dying,

I was going to school! I'm sure that was a big factor in me being able to make it in the NFL. I was not accustomed to being lax on myself.

It took discipine to excel in practice and training camp. To be able to run stadium stairs and go through drills in the heat of the summer with shoulder pads, helmets, and all that other equipment took some getting used to. But the endurance and determination I gained in being able to succeed through it were the results of disciplinary habits.

You don't always see that sort of discipline or encouragement to participate in sports today. People are focused on social media and video games instead. If a parent is not attentive, a child could be deprived of the value of hard work.

I have noticed that those who are successful find a way to get things done, and are rewarded for their hard work. I was one of the team captains in high school, but I was passed over for the all-star game because I didn't get the vote—even though I was the player of the year in my conference. I was a starter my entire career, yet I didn't get chosen as an all-star until I turned pro. My first all-star game was the Pro Bowl, and I was blessed to play in two of those games. With discipline and hard work, anything is possible. Even if it seems life isn't fair, if others are getting selected, if there's a clique or people against you, if you're demoted or passed up for something, just keep trying. Stay disciplined and your reward will come. There's a lesson in there for you, even in the adversity.

Discipline is doing what you're supposed to do, no matter what.

I remember when I was entering high school, and my parents were concerned which school I would attend. I wanted to attend a public high school because most of my friends were going there. My parents were aware that I wanted to go where the best football players and toughest guys went. But they were also aware that high school was a period in my life when everything seemed possible, even the impossible,

> **Hard work and discipline lead to strength and perseverance that cannot be replaced.**

where there would be invitations to participate in deviant behavior or activities that could destroy my chances and future opportunities. So they diverted my path to a Catholic high school instead. I've got to give my parents a lot of credit for pushing me and focusing me and striving to give me the very best. They were absolutely not going to let me fail.

Many parents today take the easy way out. Others are exemplary and take the time to spend with their kids that's needed to nurture the values and character traits we are talking about here. But for the parents who don't invest that time, imagine if you gave them this book? Imagine how those parents' mindset might change if they read about the value of pressing in and focusing on important traits that can keep their child on the right path.

High school is a time when you want to make all your dreams come true, but dreams don't come true because you wish them to do so. Dreams come true because you are committed to seeing that they do. My parents wanted me to succeed in life and wanted me to have the best opportunities in sports and education. They wanted me to be in the best environment possible for that, so they decided St. Bernard High School in Los Angeles was the best place for me.

St. Bernard was a place where academic excellence took priority over sports. I understood that my parents had my best interests at heart. In the end, St. Bernard turned out to be the top choice for me academically and socially.

At St. Bernard, some of the teachers were Catholic nuns, and the principal was a retired colonel. With him, it didn't matter who you were or what your status was among your peers; if you didn't follow the rules, you didn't play sports. It was that simple.

Once it was hard for me to discipline myself in preparation for a particular test because my focus was on Friday night's game. I didn't do well on the test. I looked forward to competing on Friday nights, but that Friday night I was not allowed to touch the field. The principal and faculty at St. Bernard helped reinforce the lesson of discipline I received at home: if you didn't do the work, you didn't get to play football. That lesson taught me the value of being disciplined through hard work. It was terrible, one of the worst moments I can remember. But it was a great lesson.

For me, letting my teammates down was enough. I never wanted that to ever happen again. I was one of the team captains. I had a responsibility to myself and my teammates to be disciplined and I had failed to discipline myself. The emotional pain of letting my teammates down was more painful than not participating in the game. My teammates placed their trust in me, and I had to make sure that I didn't disappoint them again. When you're dependable, someone can count on you to do your part.

It was through experiences such as that one at St. Bernard High School that I learned what it meant to be dependable. It was a valuable lesson in that it helped me accept the role of leadership with the responsibilities that came with it, on and off the field. No doubt, you've heard the saying, "to be a good leader you have to be a good follower." I would like to go further in saying, "to be a good follower, you must acquire what it takes to be disciplined."

At home, the lessons in being disciplined were taught within the family structure. It was the way it was going to be or you lived under another roof. My father made it clear—there were consequences in making wrong choices. If I didn't make my bed, which consisted of tucking in the sheets and pillows, there would be consequences. If I did something wrong or got a bad grade, I could not play sports.

The rules helped me understand what was important and set the right priorities in my life!

Football was just a sport I played for fun and because I enjoyed the competition. I had no idea at the

Do what you love.

time that it would blossom into a career. I started playing because of my love of the game, and that's a valuable lesson right there. Do what you love. It might just turn into the best career you've ever had. Don't choose to do something for money or do a job you hate because you're afraid of the alternative. Be wise, and be employed, but make sure you're doing whatever it is you're meant to do, and make sure you do what you love.

My parents raised us to not take any opportunity for granted. They reminded us of others who wished they had taken advantage of opportunities, or could be in our position, given the chance.

There's a reward for discipline. Throughout your life, you've been rewarded for hard work and discipline through your achievements. Think about how much better life is when you've already put in the hard work and discipline that it takes to be successful.

The most successful people in life exert personal discipline on a daily basis. To be a great and inspiring leader, you must constantly display restraint (discipline). Everyone watches what you do and draws conclusions as to your character and potential from what they see.

Not giving into something you truly want is not a weakness; it's a sign of strength. Making the right decisions in life can make or break you, and is paramount in today's hectic world. A person with discipline tends to make the right decisions. Regardless of where you exert this self-restraint, it will help promote achievement in your life.

So what can you do if you've made mistakes in this area? What do you do if you have made some bad choices? Seek coaches in your life who can help with difficult decisions, who can listen to you about

> # Change in this area will bring instant transformation.

your difficulties and provide advice. Get the right mentors who understand the obstacles you face. I challenge you to focus on increasing your discipline. Change in this area will bring instant transformation.

STEPS TO INCREASE DISCIPLINE

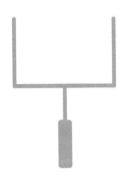

Be consistent. Focus on your goal and why you want to achieve it and then build consistent habits.

Increase your discipline by striving to be disciplined. Persistence, personal habits, and results are all intertwined.

"Hard Work"

D o you work hard or do you take the easy way out? This strategy should inspire you to think about the way you work. There are moments in sports when competition becomes the forefront of our accomplishment, when sacrifice is better than settling. A time when we possess an understanding that anything worth having is something we are going to have to pay a price to get. Hard work pays well, and it propels a lot of people to success.

What constitutes hard work to you? It is different for everyone. Each individual has a different idea or barometer of what hard work really is.

Hard work is the desire to do whatever it takes to get to the goal you have set. If we want to be successful or live our dreams, our behavior has to be in accordance with that vision. The vision of who you are and what you can do provides tremendous impact in your life. It gives your life purpose.

It has been proven that you can't wish dreams into the world of reality; you have to *create* and *produce* that reality out of what you dream. The key words here are create and produce. In order to live out your dream, you have to take action. Dreams can be a reality of what we can accomplish in life if we work hard at making them come true. Think about all the people who grew up poor, yet ended up celebrities, CEOs or millionaires because they worked their butts off to achieve their goals. Nothing big comes without a lot of sleepless nights, labor, and dedication.

My father worked for the City of Los Angeles Department of Water and Power and never missed a day of work in more than thirty years. There were times when he didn't feel like going or when he was ill, but he went to work anyway. This was the example of hard work my parents gave us. Hard work satisfies you, and not just materially, but deep within. Working gives us a sense of accomplishment and dedication. Your work ethic carries over to whatever you do in life, whether it's on the field or in the corporate world. Once my playing days were over, my work ethic transferred to the next thing I did. Work ethic is what drives us to excellence.

> # Hard work is the foundation success is built upon.

WORK HARD TO ACHIEVE YOUR GOALS.

I gained a strong understanding of hard work at an early age. I knew work was necessary to accomplish anything I attempted in life. I understood that what my parents did in their day-to-day routine took discipline. Hard work and discipline kept food on the table and a roof over my head, so it became the foundation from which I viewed the world and established my life's principles. Hard work and discipline gave me all the determination I needed. When I really saw and understood what my dad and mom had done to get me to maturity, I was determined to succeed.

My coach used to tell us that we should play the game of life the same way we approached the game of football. Our success in life depended on what we put into it. Is there any kid in high school who is not dreaming about success? In high school, I was dreaming of being successful. If being successful in football determined my success in life, then I was going to be committed to giving football everything I had.

What about you? What are you committed to? It doesn't matter if it's work or kids or a project or a sport or a new goal or business. Be committed and watch yourself succeed.

There are a lot of talented people on a team, but not everyone is a hard worker. Those who are able to combine hard work with talent become standouts; they are rewarded with an opportunity to perform on a higher level, or in a higher position.

A great coach will find ways of bringing forth the desire to work hard to meet a goal. Legendary basketball coach John Wooden taught his players how to put on their socks. It might have seemed mundane to some players. After all, who doesn't know how to put on their socks? The lesson was in the discipline of doing the smallest things correctly every time. The reason for the lesson was to keep blisters off their feet. Wooden knew that if a player got a blister, it would impact the way the player performed.

Football player and Coach Vince Lombardi began teaching his players by holding up a football and saying, "Now this is a football." He used this tactic to get players to focus on the fundamentals of the game. Once you understood the game, Lombardi moved forward to make sure you understood the concept of what it meant to work as one unit, as a team.

Herb Baum, the CEO of Dial Corporation, used to walk through the hallways serving hot dogs to his employees to show them he was dedicated to their well-being. He wanted them to know he believed in working hard and that he knew each one of them individually. Serving lunch isn't something CEOs normally do. Working hard doesn't have to be about sweat. Hard work can be about focus, effort and developing relationships, too.

Think about areas in your own life in which you want to work harder. There's a saying that goes "work smart, not hard," inferring that working hard is bad. If you can work hard, you're going to achieve much more than if you are simply smart. Do both.

Break through and ignore the myths. In society, there is a tendency to say that being a workaholic is

> # When you focus on working harder and smarter, the ultimate reward is success.

bad. But think about how many millions of people are on government subsidies or disability checks or some sort of unemployment compensation because they don't want to work. I'm not talking about people who do want to work, but can't. I'm talking about the people who do not want to work at all. Don't be like that. Be the one who strives for achievement and accomplishes great things. The truth is you can have it all. You don't have to have a poverty mentality, and you don't have to look at work as the enemy. You can show your kids and your family what a successful, hard working person is like, and you can still provide love as well as a roof over their heads. There's no nobility in poverty. If you think working hard isn't important, rethink that.

Work hard!

STRATEGY 6

"When You Lose, Don't Lose The Lesson"

How many successful people do you know who have come from humble beginnings? A lot of the smartest, most successful people in the world have come from very poor circumstances. Some were raised in orphanages or foster homes; others were raised in the projects. Success can rise from ashes. The ones who face adversity are often fighters. They had to fight to survive and they didn't have anyone doing it for them.

If you've faced a struggle in life, you know how to handle it next time. You're battle tested. You have become a warrior.

Playing sports or working as part of a business team can teach you how to handle adversity. If you carry on through struggle, it can not only change the outcome of the situation, but also teach you how to cope or how to govern yourself during moments of frustration or anger or fear. Fear can distract or cause us to lose focus.

Being able to make the right judgments, especially when you feel as if nothing matters, takes composure. Some people overcome tragedy or depression and end up changing the lives of others. Some people let their losses overtake them and go on to define themselves by those losses.

When you or perhaps the entire team loses, do you place blame or do you accept that loss, move past the defeat, and prepare for the next challenge? In business, how do you accept failure and loss? How do you deal with it when a customer takes his or her business to another competitor?

Life presents challenges, and those challenges are opportunities for self-improvement and development. Welcome the challenge and move toward it with an understanding that any challenge is an opportunity.

As a member of the team, you have opportunities for self-improvement. You are told, "Be a role model." Coaches talk about the responsibility you have to yourself and your teammates to behave accordingly when you have a goal to move toward.

As mentioned before, good character is basically who you are when no one is watching. Will you practice hard if the coach has to step away to make a phone call, or work hard when the boss is out for the day? We are able to perform well when nobody is watching only if we have good character. Take initiative. Be the one who stands out from the crowd.

Don't miss the lesson of defeat. Losing can be a good thing. It shows us where we need to improve. In competition, it is important to take time to reflect and evaluate the reasons for losing. But what about when you are doing well? It's very easy to get complacent and overlook the little things. This can happen easily. Everyone gets caught up in the excitement of the win. You are so precise in the execution of your movements, nothing can stop you. At these times, it is hard to hear advice—

especially negative feedback or constructive criticism. But we need to assess ourselves in both situations. We must learn to deal with failure, to learn lessons from our mistakes; but we also need to be able to grow even when we are doing well. Both reactions are necessary for success.

Playing a sport affords the opportunity to *trust* people outside of family or intimate friendships. Working with a team and trusting in one another toward one goal is rewarding. It develops the desire to see others succeed as well. Trust must be established in any relationship in order for it to be successful. Trust teaches us not to be threatened with fear or by the presence of competition.

Football taught me that I could experience failure and not see failure as a sign of defeat. Perhaps I just had to try harder. By focusing on the big picture, that failure or loss did not determine a season. Persevering during times of struggle and adversity produces a positive attitude; giving up produces a negative attitude. Having a positive attitude will almost always guarantee that we overcome any adversity or loss. It is certain that we will face adversity in life. It's often unexpected when adversity comes, and at times we don't get to choose it. You plan for success; you don't plan for adversity.

I remember one event in particular that could have been difficult to bounce back from. It could have sent me into a downward spiral.

I was in my second year in the NFL and we were playing a game on Christmas Eve. After the game, I was in the locker room, and someone suddenly pulled me aside and said, "You have to report to first aid." My heart skipped! My mom was in the stands that day and my mind reeled. Did she slip and fall? Break her arm? Quickly I headed to the first aid area.

I had no clue what was going on at the time. When I walked down the corridor, I noticed that people were crying, and as I got closer to the entrance of first aid, I was told that it was Lisa, my girlfriend, and not my mom. Lisa had been so supportive of my football career. She had been in the stands watching me that day. My joy over the game turned to sadness in an instant. Shockingly, Lisa died that night.

I was told that she had choked on food stuck in her windpipe. The news devastated me. It was Christmas Eve, a time to share with loved ones, and Lisa was gone. I went home that night in shock and pondered the events that had occurred in my life and my career. It was difficult for me to focus on the game during this period, but in a strange way it showed me how valuable life is.

For some, such unexpected tragedy could've ruined their career, their outlook, or their life. But for me, it made me appreciate life more. I suppose it's how you see things or choose to view them.

This was a period of growth for me.

From that moment, I understood that there are going to be periods of grief and trial. Things would not always be well with those we love. We are going to face adversity and fear. I was able to overcome tragedy at that moment because it presented an opportunity for me to concentrate on what was important. It made me aware that life is not promised to any of us; we do not know how much time we are granted on this earth. I decided that whatever I was given in terms of opportunity, I was going to make the best of it. It was what Lisa would have wanted me to do.

The death of my girlfriend taught me that although we experience pain, we have to focus forward and move on to overcome it. We have to hold ourselves accountable, even when circumstances are hard. It took discipline not to act on the frustration I felt at the time of Lisa's death.

Ultimately, life is a series of wins and losses, just like football. I learned on the field as I learned in life that you don't always win. Look at the statistics! It is impossible to think that you'll win 100% of the time because that means everyone else loses. It's how you recover from the loss that matters.

Not losing the lesson means having accountability. To really progress, you have to realize that you must claim ownership of your actions and performance. Being able to step outside yourself and objectively review your actions is what it is all about. You have to be transparent about your performance. Obviously, the goal is to improve—take what is positive and negative, and improve. Without being accountable, you always lose the lesson, and that just may be the ingredient that is missing. Being accountable can take you to a whole new level of performance.

Once you are accountable, you can establish goals and objectives to improve your performance. Goals are the building blocks of your company's vision, and tangible objectives inspire greater performance. By being accountable and transparent about your performance and by setting, tracking, and consistently evaluating progress, employees as well as teammates connect to the overall mission, become part of the culture, and make major contributions for the future.

How will you face adversity? Will you crumble when things go wrong or will you rise to the challenge and lead others to overcome? Be strong, and learn whatever the lesson is.

Being accountable is not negotiable. Individuals and organizations have an obligation to account for their activities, accept responsibility for those actions, and to disclose the results in a transparent manner. This is how business and life operate. When you lose, take a moment to reflect on the lesson you've learned. It's a test opportunity for introspection and self-reflection.

Teach others to do the same.

When we face adversity, a job loss, or a breakup, what are the lessons we can learn and take into our future? How can we grow and develop strength from the test we've just been through? It's not enough to exit a season of loss and move on. You've got to glance back, learn the lesson, and let it sharpen and strengthen you for the future.

STEPS TO APPRECIATE THE LESSONS AND ADVERSITY

Remember that there's a strength in adversity that you don't get from winning all the time. The losses and setbacks often provide the greatest stories, testimonies, and journeys. Take some time to outline some of the instances in your life when you had to overcome a hard situation. Commit those instances and the lessons they taught you to a page in your notebook. It helps us gain in clarity when we commit our lessons to paper.

Be thoughtful. Don't take a loss so hard, but search for the good in it, too. Look at a loss as a lesson.

STRATEGY 7

"Honor"

What does honor mean to you?

For some people, it means honoring their word, actions, and reputation. For others, it means honoring their family. For some people, honor isn't learned, and it's something they see displayed in others along the way.

When you're born, you have a family name; you can either honor it or not. My parents wanted me to always honor the family name. It was important to them. But honor is more than just about the family. It's about honoring yourself, and others. Even if you don't have a family, or weren't raised in one, you can honor yourself.

There were expectations given to us in our home that we were expected to meet, standards that presented us with an identity of who we were and the principles we stood on as a family unit. We were given a complete understanding of the way we should conduct ourselves at all times. It was about having a good reputation and respecting the family name.

Whenever I got into a situation at school, the very first question that came out of my parents' mouths was, "What did you do?" They didn't always automatically back me up. They wanted me to do what was right, what was honorable.

They questioned my actions first because we were given standards on how to behave in the classroom and what to do if you had a problem with anyone at school. It wasn't about choosing a side with my parents; it was always about the lesson learned.

We were at school to learn and if there were any problems, we reported it to the teacher. If we had an issue with a teacher, our job was to report that problem to mom and dad—immediately, not after we decided to deal with it our own way. Doing things your way was not encouraged in my family. There were standards, and rules set in place for us to follow that prevented us from doing things our way. We were expected to respect our family's rules, the teachers, and the student body through our behavior at school. We learned that by respecting these rules, we were honoring the family name.

This understanding became part of our outlook in life, and we learned to respect something bigger than ourselves.

Once you gain that respect in your family, on the team or in the boardroom, you must honor the position to keep that respect. You do that by holding yourself accountable to a higher standard. There are many potential Hall of Fame players who have played the game and earned the respect of their fans and their teammates, but because they didn't honor their position, their activities off the field caused them to lose that respect they earned as a player. Many have lost their careers or their positions in the game. They weren't taught honor, or they lost the lesson of honor.

It doesn't matter what your position is—you should execute that position with honor. What you do impacts people around you. You are a model, an example that others will follow, or not. Where there is respect, there is honor in the group.

I learned to respect and honor any position given to me, whether it was on a team, in my family, or in the boardroom. I had an obligation to live up to; an expectation had been made.

Honor is a thing that cannot exist with an individual alone. When it came to sports, you were taught respect for the values everyone shared as a team. That was winning!

It was an honor for me to play football and to be respected in the position I played.

When people see that you have honor, they respect you and will align their actions in accordance with yours. They see the value of putting the team's interest before their own. Soon everyone is on the same page, and when everyone is on the same page, the sky is the limit and anything is achievable.

Some people always seem to rise above their circumstances with honor, no matter what comes their way. They're well prepared, and do not allow anything to distract them from their God-given purpose. Nothing can deplete their honor. When they make mistakes, they rebound quickly because they have strong character. But they had to start somewhere, and so do you.

What do you do if you're lacking in some character traits? What if you have experienced one or two setbacks in life already? How will you handle things after that? You've got to handle adversity with a warrior mentality and a mindset of integrity. Give it your best and be honorable. Honor is conducting yourself with dignity, no matter what life throws at you.

What is your strategy to give it your best shot? How do you plan to achieve all that God has in store for you? How are you intentionally preparing for life? How are you taking responsibility for your life?

College athletics teaches players invaluable skills. With a focus on success in a particular sport, athletics is all about patience and determination. It's important to build team loyalty. These qualities go a long way toward achieving success—in the business world as well as on the field.

Circumstances occur in which decisions are made that alter people's lives forever. Haven't you ever seen someone who reacted in stress or anger and lost their legacy? A DUI arrest, a fight at a club, or some other situational circumstance derailed their dream. It's often because they didn't act with honor. Maybe they used language that wasn't right or acted in a way that dishonored their goal, or team, or dream. When you act without honor, you're dishonoring yourself. Be prepared to honor others, even when they're acting foolishly or being harsh. Choose honor and respect over retaliation and separate yourself from people who drag you down.

Remember that often we don't get to choose our team members in a given situation or job. How do you maintain sanity and honor?

If you were a pitcher for an NCAA Division I baseball team, you would have a head coach, but you would also have a special skills coach who would be 100% devoted to your pitching technique. This is not an assistant coach, but someone totally focused on helping you hone your skills in throwing a ball across home plate. This person is no different than a mentor. Find people who will help you develop the skills and character traits you want to possess.

STEPS TO FOCUS ON HONOR

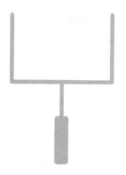

If you disagree with someone, disagree, but honor them as a human being. You can disagree without dishonoring them. You can agree to disagree and still maintain your character. When it comes to all of the principles in this book—such as honor and character and trust and setting goals for your life—a mentor can be a special guide along the journey of success.

Whatever it is you set out to do in life, do it with honor. If you don't honor the position, don't play it, because no one wants to be associated with someone who doesn't respect the company, organization, or team. They respect those who bring honor to the position they are given. Honor is a position of respect. Be honorable.

STRATEGY 8

"COURAGE"

When was the last time you had to demonstrate courage in your own life? Everyone has moments where they need to dig deep and make adjustments, and sometimes it means facing big fears. This is when courage comes into play. I could go on and on about the courage it takes to face a gigantic player on the other side of the field, but I can think of a lot more challenging situations.

Courage is something that comes naturally to some people, but takes work for others. If you've ever witnessed someone fighting a health battle or dealing with a life-threatening diagnosis, you may have seen courage. If you've watched someone deliver a big speech or presentation to a roomful of people, you've witnessed a different kind of courage. Making the decision to be courageous means stepping up when you don't necessarily want to. Courage is not giving up, but pushing through your fears with strength and hope.

Courage means to have strength in your mind to never give in despite the odds. It is being able to speak out against unfairness when no one else will. It's an inner strength that gives us the ability to endure adversity or pain. Courage is needed to advance, to be inspired, and to overcome. How can you be encouraged, if you are without courage?

When I joined Vanderbilt University as the Director of Player Development, it was a new adventure. Doesn't every new venture require courage?

You don't know what you're facing. But you know you've got to get up every morning and show up, suit up and inspire and lead. You've got a choice. Will I be courageous or will I be hesitant and uncertain? I choose confidence and courage.

The *Harvard Business Review* wrote an article about courage as a business skill and how we can work to develop it more. It described courage as "calculated risk taking." When you're faced with a challenge, it may be courage that takes you through it. Courage can be harnessed in different ways in different situations.

Everyone possesses the opportunity for courage. Some become like the cowardly lion in the Wizard of Oz, looking for something they already possess. And like the lion, many of us don't know we have courage until we are put in a position to face what we fear. Courage means to have strength in your mind to never give up in spite of the odds.

The acquisition of courage begins with determination. If we are determined to achieve what we set out to do, we will develop courage along the way because we are not afraid of failure. Courage doesn't mean you won't have fear or anxiety. It just means you'll push through and go that extra mile.

Malcolm X said, "A man who believes in freedom will do anything under the sun to acquire it." That's courage. Courage means to overcome fear and do whatever is necessary to get what you want.

Before every game, I had to learn to overcome fear, or at the very least, a case of the "butterflies." In sports we called it butterflies because of the flutters you get in your gut before you walk onto the field. If you ever played sports, you know what I'm talking about. There's a jumpiness that's brought on by your desire to perform well. What I learned to do was to turn that fear into fire.

Whenever I felt butterflies before the game, I meditated on the reason I was there. I was there to win, and I was determined to win each time I stepped onto the field. Whenever I brought that determination into focus, my fear turned to fire. I got a boost of adrenaline toward accomplishing the goal. I was ready to play. I was going to do what was necessary for the team to be successful.

Courage is easier to obtain when you have an important reason for it. No one is going to be courageous unless they believe in something. Again, for leaders, this is paramount, because if you can inspire and motivate your team to an action-oriented, value-based mission, they'll be more likely to act courageously. They'll have courage when faced with any problems because they believe in what they are doing. They'll be courageous in their presentations against your competition and they'll have the courage to tell you the truth.

> **Some people fail to develop the skill of turning fear into fire.**

The strongest business cultures and organizations are built on courage. When you think of the Marines, or the Navy Seals, or business organizations that thrive on truth and operate on strength and transparency, you think of the courageous individuals who work there. Think of the courage of emergency room doctors, or the courage of soldiers in a battle. They stand united against an opposition that is greater than anything they could combat alone as an individual. They muster up the courage and strength to carry on.

Courage takes a unique and positive attitude.

It's a trait that you get from playing sports, but if you think about it, you can aspire to it under any circumstance. Many people possess the will to attempt something, but not the courage to accomplish it. I've seen this with teammates. Some teammates lose their will to play in the third or fourth quarter because the game seems to get out of reach.

Pep talks don't work as a motivator because you can't encourage where courage doesn't exist. Courage is something different. Your will says to attempt it, but real courage says to continue to push until there is no reason to push further.

If my opponent was bigger or stronger, I met that force with a greater effort. Doing this developed skills that would allow me to gain the upper hand whenever I was overmatched. I discovered you can do more and accomplish more if you never give up. I never gave up.

I developed this attitude from hard work and discipline. Whenever I trained, I developed endurance from that training. That endurance and the discipline in my work ethic created in me the strength I needed to carry on when I was tired, injured, or just plain done. To me, that was the time to turn it up, to muster the strength to finish the game the same way I started it.

Once you learn to step into courage and away from fear, anything is possible. You don't need to see a wizard to understand it. All you have to do is turn and face your fears. Turn that fear into fire. Many people fear the unknown, and the outcome of any undertaking that's uncertain. Butterflies will come before a game, an interview, or the first day on the job. It's a natural fear of the unknown mixed with our desire to perform well in the task at hand. But if we are determined to accomplish what we set out to do, courage develops within us and we approach whatever the task is with confidence. We step out of fear and turn that fear into fire.

The world has produced leaders who had the courage to stand up for what was right and lead others to do the same. They were not afraid of doing something even though it was difficult. You've got to try.

Everybody wants a raise, or the corner office. Everybody wants to be successful. Kevin Hart, the comedian, says, "Everybody wants to be famous, but nobody wants to put in the work." To be successful, you have to work. To endure the struggles along the path, you're going to need courage—the confidence to act in accordance with what you believe you can accomplish. Find courage, and be encouraged that anything is possible.

STEPS TO ENHANCE YOUR COURAGE

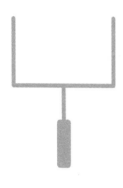

Take inventory of your fears and face them. In what ways can you be more courageous?

The first step is awareness!

Focus on building courage to motivate yourself in greater ways. There are many ways to develop personal courage. The first way is to encourage your soul. Make a habit of reading the personal testimonies of those who have faced giants in their lives and won.

Begin to recognize what your own giants are. How can you overcome them and face them with courage?

STRATEGY 9

"HUMILITY"

he most talented human in the world is worthless if they're arrogant. Arrogance is a toxin.

One of the lessons that stuck with me while playing sports was not to be arrogant. I learned this lesson from my parents and coaches, and each taught me in their own way. My mother said to me, "You don't have to brag. If you are doing what you're supposed to do, people will brag for you." My coaches told us our performance was measured by what we did on the field, which said to me that talking didn't win games.

I carried these lessons with me throughout the course of my career. I never bragged about myself, my achievements, or my abilities. I realized that words didn't matter because people judge you on your performance, what you do on the field. Humility allowed me to focus on improving. I never thought I was the best; I always felt I needed to improve or that I could get better.

Having an attitude to always do your best propels your efforts, and your life, to greatness. If you shoot for the moon and miss, at least you'll rest among the stars. Anybody can talk, but can you produce? This is the thinking in the business world. Your success depends upon whether or not you can be productive in the work environment. To be productive, you have to be willing to work alongside others. Arrogance and success don't mix.

I learned humility from the discipline I got at home and in school. Both were instrumental to me adopting a humble mindset. I was not better than other people. If I didn't do well in school, there were consequences at home and in school. I was punished at home, and had to miss Friday games at school. Those were the consequences I faced. I learned to humble myself. Humility kept the doors of opportunity open.

I came to the conclusion that I wasn't better than anyone else when I didn't make the all-star team in high school. I was one of the best players in the conference. When the votes came down, I didn't get enough votes, so I was not included. That was a humbling experience for me.

I didn't bad-mouth the selection committee or belittle anyone who was chosen to play in the game. I used the rejection as motivation, as a sign I needed to improve. It wasn't personal. I just needed to play better. Humility offers and welcomes improvements in your life. Who among us doesn't need to improve in some aspect of our lives? In order to advance, we must improve, right?

Humility helped me stay grounded. I made a choice after the all-star incident to continue working harder. The next time—if there was a next time—I would position myself to get the votes I needed to be an all-star. I completed my career in the NFL as a two time Pro Bowler and first-time, first-team All-Pro. I would not have earned those accolades if I hadn't learned the lesson of humility out of the all-star experience in high school. That episode helped me to accept constructive criticism, and to improve when I needed to get better.

The toughest thing for most people to accept is negative feedback. Most of us are content with the amount of success we have in life. We don't feel we need to improve, but we still desire the corner office, the starting role, or the leadership position. Acquiring those positions in life has a great deal to do with improving character. Being humble helps in this area.

Humility helps you recognize what you need to improve. It welcomes change when we become disappointed with the way things are going, and that leads to improvement. Humility helps us to look at reality. We understand that to change our situation, we have to change ourselves and perhaps our outlook on the situation. We must improve for things to get better.

I was taught that your fate is in your own hands, that what you do in life will determine the amount of success you have. What can you add to your life, bring to a company, or do for a team that will in return bring success into your life? You have to be willing to learn what that contribution is.

Humility will open a door for you to discover even more of your gifts and talents. It helped me discover what I needed to do to be successful in the business world.

When an employer calls you in for an interview, they are not only looking at whether you can do the job. They've got training programs for that. They can teach an individ-

> **If you think you already know, you will never find out.**

ual to do the job. They are more interested in whether you have to be taught to work well with others, or if you can humble yourself to the way they do things. Will you be a good contribution to the team? Will you be viewed as an asset? Or will you be viewed as an arrogant wild card who only talks about his or her own accomplishments?

Companies don't care about how you did things at your last job; most companies have their own system. To learn that system, you have to approach your new job with humility. Nobody wants to work with a person who acts like a know-it-all their first day on the job. The know-it-all will only do things one way—their way. The know-it-all doesn't welcome an opportunity to improve or learn. This type of person views criticism as a personal attack. The know-it-all will never work well as a teammate because that takes humility.

Working as a team is rewarding. You gain a lot of respect and friendship. Being humble gives you an advantage because you enter the work environment and you are easily welcomed by your peers. Humility encourages teamwork among the group. Companies see humility as a valuable asset. This is why humility is so important for the leadership position. It doesn't matter if you're the leader on a team or the CEO of a company. People are not motivated by arrogance.

If you have ever been in an environment where the leadership or management displayed arrogance in character, you've suffered the consequences. It's frustrating to experience. The group will not honor that person or the position they hold. When the leadership feels that their position is more important than everyone else's, those who perform the duties that make the company or team successful don't want to follow that leader. This is followed by gossip, backstabbing leadership, or disorder among the group. Group morale goes down, and so does the production. Let's face it—there are people who will decide they don't want to work for you if you're an arrogant leader. If they do put up with you, they won't work as hard, or they'll constantly undermine your success.

If a leader yells, criticizes, and blames others, it will be hard for them to humble themselves, simply because of their arrogance.

Arrogance can kill the motivation of a team or company. It will discourage unity and teamwork.

Humility is an attribute you must possess in the corporate world. Your success is not acknowledged in the same way that it would be when you're a rock star or a standout player on the field. You can't dance in the touchdown zone or spout off on the basketball court. In sports, if you score a touchdown, make a goal or cause a game winning turnover, everybody sees it, and everybody cheers. In the business environment, there are no cheerleaders. Your accomplishments are under the table, and often go unnoticed. Only a few people know what you contribute for the success of the company. Sometimes, it can feel as if you're not getting rewarded or recognized at all.

In sports, if you're a good player and you're not playing, many spectators have their own opinion about the situation. In many cases, fans' opinion can matter. In the corporate world, there is no such scrutiny. In the corporate world, there are no spectators—just a hierarchy that you have to report to. What matters is the image of the company. The business is neither aware of nor concerned about your personal performance on the team. Management is focused on the reputation of the company.

Humility is what allows you to continue your success on the job without expecting that pat on the back, the cheers from the crowd. It takes humility to perform to the highest standard and to be secure, knowing that your work ethic and efforts are appreciated.

Humility comes from the ability to admit your mistakes. Some of our most significant successes in life and in business come from mistakes that we have made and learned from. One's ability to remain open to learning from mistakes and to receiving constructive criticism is the key to making significant positive strides and achieving long-term success. Of all of God's many directives, one of the most important is to stay humble. In fact, without humility, why would we obey any of God's other commandments? No matter what your belief system, humility is an attractive trait.

In today's global marketplace, no one will have all the answers. Staying humble may be one of the most important virtues you can have to achieve success today.

Studies show humility as one of four critical leadership factors for creating an environment where employees from different demographic backgrounds feel included. One study that surveyed more than 1,500 workers from Australia, China, Germany, India, Mexico, and the U.S. found that when employees observed selfless managerial behavior, characterized by acts of humility, those employees were more likely to report feeling included in their work teams. This was true for both women and men.

Continuing to stay humble and valuing input about areas where performance could improve is key and a priority for any success-focused person. Humility drives an attitude of acceptance and can singlehandedly take one to new levels of performance.

Martin Luther King, Jr. asked a group of junior high school students, "What is your life's blueprint?" He went on further, saying, "And when you discover what you will be in your life, set out to do it as if God Almighty called you at this particular moment in history to do it. Don't just set out to do a good job. Set out to do such a good job that the living, the dead, or the unborn couldn't do it any better...If you can't be a pine at the top of the hill, be a shrub in the valley. Be the best little shrub on the side of the hill. Be a bush if you can't be a tree. If you can't be a highway, just be a trail. If you can't be a sun, be a star. For it isn't by size that you win or fail. Be the best of whatever you are."

If you are self-centered, you'll feel like you have to be recognized for the things that you do. Your chances of success in the business world will probably be slim to none. In the business world, you're not always going to get that pat on the back. You have to be self-motivated and humble; these traits will allow you to perform your duties with honor regardless of recognition. Bragging will not help you in any way in the real world.

When I played football, I understood that when an opponent trash talked, he was trying to intimidate me, put fear in me. I learned to turn that fear into fire by understanding that the opponent spoke that way because he respected me as a worthy foe. He was trying to convince me of his own success. I was concerned about my success, not his! My mom told me that whenever I encountered success. I should act like I'd never been there before. Someone who is unsure of their ability will work hard at convincing others that they can be successful; eventually they will come to believe it themselves. Be humble and confident on your way to success.

You have to believe in your own capabilities. When you become sure of your potential, you won't have to convince others; they'll see it for themselves. If you believe you can be successful, you will be successful. When you are, act like you've never been there before. It will only open the door for more success to come your way, because you are humble.

STEPS TO INCREASE HUMILITY

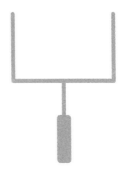

Be aware. Ask yourself, am I humble and grateful?

Not everyone can handle success the same way. Success destroys the lives of many because they weren't ready for it. Success changes some people because they forgot what it took to get there. My advice is to learn what it means to be humble along the way.

Being humble is a quiet strength, not a weakness. Look at leaders like Nelson Mandela. He had a quiet strength that people admired. You don't always need to be loud about your achievements. Just show up, and let your preparation and performance and character speak for you. All of these traits are intertwined. All of these traits add up to personal growth, self-improvement, and leadership.

STRATEGY 10

"PREPARATION"

ow prepared are you for success?

Preparation is the process of making yourself ready for opportunity. It is the difference between taking chances and grasping an opportunity. If you're not prepared, you can miss the opportunity.

You probably know people who talk about their missed chances in life. They say, "I had a chance to do this or that, but...". That "but" was the thing that prevented them from grasping what could have been their once-in-a-lifetime, golden opportunity. At least that's what they say.

What you don't hear is, "I wasn't prepared." They don't tell you how or why they missed the opportunity. Preparation is the process by which you decide how you're going to perform or execute a task. Part of preparing is envisioning how you'll perform with your abilities and tools before you do it. Everyone talks about success, but not everyone is prepared for it. Success requires hard work. There are no shortcuts. To acquire success, you have to be prepared for the undertaking. This involves planning. If you don't plan at succeeding, you put yourself in a position for failure.

In sports, you learn to prepare for your opponent. When you are prepared, it makes you stronger, and allows you to exploit the other team's weaknesses. Preparation adds to your capabilities. What would it be like if you didn't rely simply on your talents, but actually prepared mentally to win long before you had to compete? It would make all the difference.

Preparation is the key to success. The more I prepared, the better I performed. The better I performed, the more I advanced with each opportunity. Coaches told me, "You'll play like you practice and practice like you play." It is the same in life. You get out of it what you put into it. Your effort will determine your value to your company or team.

When I was drafted into the NFL, there were at least three other guys drafted to play the same position. And I wasn't the first pick. In the pros, you're an all-star among all-stars. A lot of players get to this level and forget the work ethic it took to get there. Because they stop working on their abilities, they are not successful on the professional level.

Preparation determines who performs well consistently.

When you make an effort toward preparation, you plan for the unimaginable, the impossible. You ready yourself for the challenge and you're able to change or adjust yourself to make the best effort. You become a game changer. Your preparation allows you to decide how you are going to perform before you do it. You're always thinking a step ahead. You discover techniques and methods that allow you to position yourself in the right place, at the right time.

This preparation is similar to the process used in studying for a test. To pass a test, you need to study. One's preparation for the test makes all the difference. Studying was a key to my success in football and in the business world. To win in football, we had to examine our opponent, and to have success in the world, we have to examine our life.

What if you prepared for 99% of the obstacles or opposition you could possibly face before you delivered a presentation at work? Your answers would come naturally because they were internalized. You'd be adept and prepared to handle and overcome any challenge.

Preparing gives you the necessary endurance to perform at a higher level. You have a plan, a blueprint of what's going to grant you success; you've thought about all the possibilities. Sometimes, the blueprint comes from someone else. All that matters is that it works. What has proven to work for someone else can also work for you. It just has to be tested in your life. I learned methods from others who were successful.

What happens when you win without ever preparing? That's not a bad thing when it occurs. But don't count on it. Prepare for opportunities.

There are some people in the corporate world who are not qualified for the positions they have because they never prepared. They knew somebody, or knew somebody who knew somebody else who helped them get the job. When somebody gives you a job you didn't earn, it alienates you in the group. Everyone around you is aware that you are not supposed to be there. It's not that they envy the position you're in; they just know you're not qualified for it. In those situations, you've got to work harder and perform better to earn respect. Sometimes we are blessed with opportunities we don't deserve; we should prepare then, too, so we might be worthy of the responsibility we've been given.

I've made mistakes in life, and I must reiterate that it pays to have good mentors around you. In high school, I wasn't expecting to play football in the NFL. It was preparation that got me there. Once I got to the NFL, I knew I wasn't going to play for the rest of my life. I knew I needed something to fall back on. I had to work to be afforded an opportunity to play on the highest level in sports. I utilized the same methods to be successful in the business world.

> **If you want success, prepare for it.**

Preparation is the key to success and to continued success. If you want success, prepare for it. In the NFL, when a guy gets released by a team, his face turns to stone. A lifelong dream has ended. I've seen guys shed tears because their dreams have been shattered. You can't go into a different career with no experience, but many players don't understand that. In the pros, you have to constantly improve, but with a focus on football, a player can be prepared for the game, but not for the real world.

There are many guys who don't want to leave the sports world. Their whole focus is their career, and they are not thinking about what they will do after it is over. They don't prepare mentally or financially for the inevitable. We have to prepare ourselves for life. You don't realize the talents you have until you tap into the world of the unknown.

STEPS TO BEING PREPARED

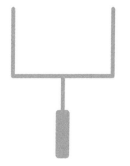

Are there ways you could be better prepared? Live your life intentionally. Examine your schedule with your mentor and build this strategy into your life.

"LEADERSHIP"

Be a leader and not a follower. When you're young, you may not understand the consequences of some of the choices you make. But as you mature, you start to see the results. Leadership is a decision. It's a choice you make.

Everyone possesses leadership potential, but many aren't aware of it. You've got to learn how to lead. Sometimes you even lead before you learn how. Make the decision to be

> ## Whether you develop as a follower or a leader in life depends on you.

a leader! A leader becomes a leader by his or her example. The example that others see. My first example of leadership was from my father. He went to work every day, and fixed things around the house. He was consistent in the lessons he taught me as a child. The primary lesson he taught me was not to rely on others to do your work for you. I also learned leadership from mentors, coaches, and teachers. They helped me discover my own potential to become a leader.

To develop leadership potential, you have to accept mentors in your life. It's important to have people around us who will advise us on the choices we make. Having mentors helped me understand the importance of setting a good example. People are motivated in different ways. What motivates some may not motivate others. Some are motivated by a direct approach and others may be motivated by what you do. Some people are motivated when the group accomplishes a goal, or when the team scores a touchdown. Learning what motivates people is the key to being successful as a leader.

A good leader understands that confidence is a factor to success. Self-assurance is what attracts people to your leadership potential. In sports, many people are confident, but won't assume the role of a leader. Even so, the confidence they show may attract or influence others to follow the example they set.

Being a leader is more than holding a position of respect. It is also about holding yourself accountable in your actions. If you are a leader, others will naturally follow you. It doesn't matter if you are a parent or a sports figure or a manager or the owner of a business—people will judge you by your example. If you're not setting a good example, they will not respect you as a leader. Each of us takes on a leadership role in one way or another in our lives, so we should be careful to set a good example and always strive to improve.

A good leader should be a good listener. My high school coach used to tell me, "If you're going to lead, be a quiet leader." You've probably heard the saying that we have two ears and one mouth, meaning we should listen more and talk less. Listening invites understanding. Anytime an understanding is reached, it becomes an element for progress, whether it be in conversation, a relationship, or on the job. If we develop the quality of being good listeners, it will help us be better leaders.

Leadership is something that shouldn't be taken for granted. It is an honor, and an opportunity that will create other opportunities. When you are a leader, you have to accept the responsibility that comes with the position. People are watching. Your abilities will be tested, and when they are, you must respond to the best of those abilities. When in a crisis, or when the team is on a losing streak, or when others are trying to lead others down the wrong path, you have to make the best decisions possible. An effective leader has the courage to make tough decisions as well as easy ones. Leadership requires courage!

When I was a rookie in the pros, quarterback Warren Moon was our team's leader. I learned how to be an effective leader by observing him. I watched how he handled the media and how he addressed team issues. Because I was a starter my first year in the league, I had to step into a leadership role very quickly. Warren Moon offered examples and advice on how to be an effective leader on the team. The example he set and the values by which he lived also apply in business. Inside the corporate world, it's important to be the best leader you can be, no matter what level you're on or what role you're serving in.

Being a leader means making a commitment to success. What's your leadership strategy? Maybe it's to focus on becoming a better leader in your own family, or becoming a stronger public speaker, or to read more self-improvement books like this one! Leadership is a growth process. That's the good news. You can always learn and grow and become even sharper than you already are.

Most people underestimate what a mentor can do to help. They believe a mentor is a negative thing, someone who may have too much control. This is the biggest reason for failure in business, sports, and in life. A mentor offers valuable insight in dealing with obstacles and challenges along the way. People call this experience. A mentor will use experience, understanding, and knowledge to teach and provide insight into a matter that you may not be familiar with. Sometimes the mentor has already paid the price in a similar situation and is in a perfect position to offer the wisdom of experience, if you need it.

With a strong mentor, you will have someone in your corner knowledgeable about your endeavors, actions, goals, or business. I can't stress the importance of this. If you don't yet have a mentor, you better find one before you need one. A mentor is more than a friend. It's someone who can guide you intelligently through solutions.

Sometimes a mentor is more like a cheerleader, offering continued support and encouragement. A mentor will always will tell you the truth. You have family and friends you can lean on, but many times, those closest to you will not tell you the bad news or hard things that you must know to achieve your goals. Friends are friends. They have your happiness in mind. A mentor is more than that. A mentor is one who has your growth in mind.

Go over your leadership skill list with you mentor, and let that mentor guide you as you grow.

STEPS TO INCREASE LEADERSHIP SKILLS:

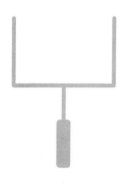

Ask other leaders for feedback on ways you can develop leadership skills.

Take a leadership class, read leadership books, and most of all, become a leader. Make the decision to be proactive instead of reactive. Leaders are action-oriented.

Make a decision to be results-focused. What are the best results for the team? Leaders develop and enhance others.

Make a decision to be a mentor to someone else.

STRATEGY 12

"ATTITUDE"

ow's your attitude?

You can sense the attitude of most people the moment you meet them. Have you ever met someone who had a bad attitude or a victim mentality? Their attitude follows them like a bad smell. No one wants to be around someone who always has a bad attitude.

Attitude is contagious. Have you ever noticed how an individual with a positive attitude seems to engage

Attitude is contagious.

everyone around them? That's the great thing about positive attitudes. You can get one for free just by making the decision to have it. Great leaders understand how to have a good attitude. They hire people with great attitudes.

Your attitude involves your beliefs, and how you feel; it is your general outlook on life. Are you the kind of person who has a positive attitude in any given situation or do you always expect the worst? Possessing a positive outlook many times leads to a favorable outcome.

Sports can produce the positive attitude we need to succeed in life. In sports, everybody wants to be victorious. Having a desire to win creates a good attitude in an individual; it teaches them to believe that success in any endeavor is possible. Our attitude will determine how far we go in life. If we can't control our attitude, we hinder our chances at success.

My attitude can enhance a situation. Many people let their attitude get the best of them; how they handle a situation can hinder their opportunity or limit their success. They let their emotions dictate their decisions, instead of making decisions based on a positive attitude. There are those who are content one moment, but cannot handle adversity. They counter problems with a poor attitude and pass those negative feelings on to everyone else! Don't be that person. Adopt a positive attitude.

Don't be reactive to situational success. Have a measure of control about your responses, and you'll start to see your attitude change! Think about it this way: If we respond to situations negatively, the results will be negative, which will hinder our own chances at success. Having a good attitude will bring good results in your life.

When I played sports, there were players who couldn't control their attitude when someone said something to them. That's like being a toddler. If the coach didn't give them enough playing time or if another player mouthed off to them, they mouthed off right back.

Have you ever had that in your life? Some people have a pattern of losing jobs, or relationships, because they lack self-control. They respond to criticism with vulgar words or by fighting. That's a very low level of thinking. Leaders don't do that. Leaders lead in the face of adversity. Leaders control their attitude and actions and words, and make a bad situation better.

Some players get bad attitudes because they feel they have been wronged. They respond negatively to the situation and ultimately hinder their own chances of playing in the next game, or even staying on the team! Talk about ruining your own life because you have no self-control.

If you have a pattern of losing your temper, go back to the moment when you first experienced conflict. How did you respond? Look back and learn from it. If you have a habit of arguing or responding with anger, you may want to practice some self-control. Some people justify their behavior patterns by saying, "Well, I wasn't supposed to be there anyway." But if you notice, they do it over and over again because they've never identified the pattern or their own responsibility in the conflict.

You have to change how you feel toward unfavorable situations in life. Choosing to maintain a positive attitude while going through difficulty helps you overcome and learn how to govern yourself in those moments.

Attitude is linked to outcome.

My attitude was very important when playing sports. In fact, it was strongly linked to my actions and

Attitude is linked to outcome.

determined my success. A person who has a pessimistic attitude toward winning will not give as much effort as a person with a positive attitude. The pessimist doesn't have the desire to carry on if the outcome is unfavorable. They adopt a "what's-the-use?" attitude when real effort is needed to get back in the game. But a person with a positive attitude will give everything they've got until the game is over. I was going to play my heart out, no matter what, in every game I played. This attitude carried over in everything I did. It carried over into the business world, and my home. I was going to finish the job the best I could. Having this positive attitude changed my life. A positive attitude produces a favorable outcome. Whether it is a meeting, job, sports, or a date, you only have one chance to make a first impression. Your attitude will determine that impression.

Attitude impacts performance in business and life. It determines how we approach a given situation. In sports, the attitudes of the players are factors in whether or not they will be victorious. Similarly, in business, the attitudes of workers determine their success. Jeffrey J. Fox wrote in his book on how to be a superstar marketer that "some people get in business or are in business to say they have a business. Some people are in business for success and to stay in business. Which one are you?"

Are you the type of person who brings their talents to the table but lets their negative attitude get in the way of reaching their goal? Or are you the one who brings a positive attitude and the right talents to the table? A positive attitude will almost ensure your success. A negative attitude will almost ensure your lack of it.

If you're the new guy on the team, having a positive attitude will also ensure you are welcomed among your teammates. It will help you offer healthy teamwork and support, even if you're not doing real well. In sports or business, a good attitude will produce harmony in a group or among teammates. Everyone will adapt to the standards set in the group and take responsibility in seeing that those standards are kept. People love to see a good person do well. They will support you on your way to success.

Abraham Lincoln said, "We can complain because rose bushes have thorns, or rejoice because thorn bushes have roses." You can either focus on the rose or the thorns!

How's your attitude? What can you do to help yourself maintain healthy attitudes at work?

STEPS TO A POSITIVE ATTITUDE

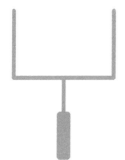

Wake up each day with a positive word for yourself. Train your mind and heart in positive ways.

Read positive things, and stay focused on having a good attitude.

Make a commitment to developing your internal positive attitude by monitoring the words you say to yourself. It's as important as what you say to others.

Attitude is what you create in your own mind. You can turn heaven into hell or hell into heaven. Renew your own mind. Romans 12:2 says, "Do not conform to the pattern of this world, but be transformed by the renewing of your own mind".

"RESPECT"

I n life and in business, respect is earned.

Respect is an unselfish gesture that earns us the privilege of being worthy of it. It involves observing others, giving your best, behaving properly, being courteous, and accepting differences. These are all qualities of a person who carries themselves with respect.

Having the consideration to listen even when you're not interested, or to open a door for someone, or

> **Respect means to have a healthy regard and concern for others, or to give others your attention when called for.**

to submit to those who are in authority over you, are other examples of being respectful. We learn respect from those around us and our mentors.

The first place we learn about respect is in the home. My parents taught us that talking while someone else was carrying on a conversation was not respectful to the person who was talking. Talking back to elders, teachers, coaches or anyone in authority over you was also considered disrespectful. It brought dishonor to the family name.

Learning the lesson of respect is valuable because you carry it with you when you leave your home. Learning to respect your elders teaches you to humble yourself to coaches or mentors who are older than you. You automatically give them the respect they deserve due to their position.

Having respect for others welcomed mentors into my life. I found that mentors didn't want to waste their time where it was not appreciated. Mentors seek to encourage those who want or have shown potential for success in what they're doing. An individual who has no respect for themselves or others may have the desire to be successful, but our success is determined by how others view us.

Athletes can be viewed as successful among their teammates and fans, but when they do something that shows disrespect for their position or themselves, others do not want to help them as much as they did before. They can lose endorsements or get demoted. Their teammates and peers may also begin to resent them.

How many times have we seen CEOs, pastors, politicians, or celebrities lose respect because of a scandal? It may have been poor behavior, an affair, drug use, or something else they weren't supposed to be doing, but they lost the respect of those who had supported them. Respect is won or lost depending upon your behavior.

Make a commitment to respect others and yourself.

When people don't respect you, they won't support you, either. If no one supports your goals, they become more difficult to reach. What about those who have no respect for order? They are viewed in society as vicious, unpredictable, and reckless. Is this the way you want others to see you?

In order to grow and become a better leader, respect must be part of your DNA. All of the rules and life lessons in this book fit together to help each of us grow. They overlap a lot, which you have probably noticed. Leadership involves attitude, and attitude determines the results, and the results depend on respect, leadership, and your ability to overcome adversity and every obstacle in your path. All of this contributes to your success in life.

People struggle with respect because sometimes there are individuals in positions of power who shouldn't be there. Don't be disrespectful to this individual. Just do what you have to do until this bad leader moves on, because they will.

You don't have to like an individual to show them respect. I teach my son (who is now playing football and basketball) that he will have coaches or teachers that he might not like. He might not like the way these leaders do everything, but in order to earn respect as a member of the team, he has to respect their leadership position anyway. Signs of disrespect are viewed by scouts, coaches, and teammates as evidence that you are not coachable. If you're not coachable, it means you can't be trained or taught. We've all heard of loudmouthed, abusive players who are difficult to work with. They end up getting traded repeatedly until their career is finally spent, and no one remembers them with anything approaching admiration. No one wants to be like them.

There are a lot of good athletes with talent, but respect overrides talent. When you are respectful, people understand they can work with you. When you can work along with others, you can be a useful part of a team because you understand teamwork. Respect is required among teammates and associates.

What happens when there's no mutual respect? Sometimes you see a player in business or sports who is a talented trailblazer, but who doesn't respect others. This mismatch is devastating to a career. Even prison guards have to earn respect from the inmates in order to not get jumped. In the corporate world, respect must be earned in order to get things accomplished. You don't simply rise to the next level without respect. What are some ways you can learn to give and receive respect? Don't forget that you have to give it to get it.

STEPS TO CULTIVATE RESPECT

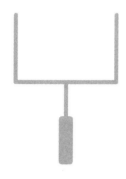

If I were teaching this concept to a group of young men or mentoring others on this step, I'd give them the following tips:

1. Learn to listen: Take time to listen to others, whether it's about your game or just an observation. Don't be defensive.

2. Get a mentor you can trust to really help you decipher and interpret feedback. Mentors are great at helping you separate the message from the messenger. Sometimes the way feedback is delivered overshadows the actual points the person is trying to make; a good mentor can help you sort that out.

3. Don't overreact. You cannot control what some people say or think about you, but you can control how you react. Own that and take care to keep things in perspective. Don't let your feelings spiral out of control. You always want to be moving forward. Backing up is not progress.

STRATEGY 14

"TRUST"

Most adults realize that trust is the basis for all relationships, in life and in business. Trust is something you build and constantly prove and reaffirm. Trust is critical with clients, with friends, and with family. When someone close to you comes to you with a problem, can they trust that you'll protect their confidence and not share it with strangers? When your client comes to you for solutions, can they trust that you'll care about their issues enough to fight for resolutions? Trust is everything. I remember a time on the field when I had a teammate I didn't trust. Everything was more difficult. He felt that his individual success was more important than anything else. It took long talks and some self-discovery for him to realize that his value went up exponentially as the team was more successful. You see it every year. Players from the Super Bowl are sought after the most.

Trust makes a team work. In business, you've got to trust your colleagues to get the job done and support your ideas. Trust is also critical to the way families bond and grow. If a parent is abusive, either verbally or physically, the child learns that he or she cannot trust that their parent won't respond with anger. To deal with that, the children start keeping secrets. Trust is not just about telling the truth; it's also defined by our consistency in words and actions.

We need to know who we can trust. I learned to put my trust in God. My parents taught us and led us into having a relationship with God like He was a member of the family. As we grew, we were taught the importance of being conscious of God. He saw our every move and judged us accordingly. He loved us. When all was done here on earth, His acceptance was critical. God helped us develop into trustworthy individuals who wanted to please Him. I was raised in a Catholic home that had God as its center. I understood trust to be the true essence of a person; their ability to walk in trust was the foundation for their character. You know what they would do if no one was watching—they would be true.

We learn our first lessons about trust at very young age. It doesn't matter if that family consists of biological parents or members of an extended family—trust is learned from those who raise you. In those lessons we learn who and who not to trust.

When people trust you, they believe what you have told them. They believe you have the ability you claim you have, that you are capable of upholding your end of an agreement. We place confidence in something we trust. It tests self-assurance. Trust is something you learn or earn, but it can be broken. Broken trust results in broken hearts and is devastating to all parties.

Broken trust destroys opportunities, causes separation, and creates a bad situation. When you get hurt, a healing process has to take place before that trust can be reestablished. No one really escapes this; there has to be closure. That means each person has to accept responsibility for their own choices or they may not be able to trust or be trusted again.

If your trust has been broken, how do you shift your focus? Do you focus on the situation or the individual? It doesn't matter if you are the betrayer or the one who has been betrayed in a relationship, or as a member of an organization. What caused the breach—the situation, the individual, or the choice that was made? The answers to these questions will help you grow and reestablish trust.

We make most of our decisions because we trust in a favorable outcome or positive results. Trust plays a necessary role in life; without it, we are fighting a losing battle. You have to trust others and others have to know they can trust you. Trust is essential when it comes to success.

In football, everyone has to know their job on the field. You have confidence that they can trust you. Everyone understands that if they do their job, the goal can be achieved. Each member is accountable to doing what they said they would do. You do your job and not someone else's.

During my career, I saw superstars who came to a new team. There was talk about what they did on another team, and how they were going to perform. When the new team went on a losing streak, the superstars tried to do everybody else's jobs for them. This caused a breakdown on the team, and the team not only lost games, but a lack of trust developed among the team members because they weren't being trusted to do their jobs. Trust gets tested. Telling someone you don't trust them is the same as telling them you don't want them around you. You can put talented people together on a team, but if each is not holding themselves accountable for the duties they're entrusted with, there will be a breakdown in trust and their efforts will result in failure. People do not perform well around individuals they can't trust. This is why it's important to surround yourself with people you trust.

In the pros, I had a roommate and friend named Curtis. He was a guy I could trust. Like me, he was a Christian. Curtis not only talked the talk, he walked the walk—on and off the field. The blossoming of his career influenced mine. He was the type of person who always showed up when called upon. He never compromised his beliefs to gain fame or popularity. By watching his example, I learned how to keep my balance when faith brings favor. Curtis and I both believed that we could do all things through Christ. (Philippians 4:13)

Because we trusted God, there was no need to find other methods to gain favor. There were times when we hung out with other teammates who were drinkers and accustomed to profane language, but when they were with us, they acted differently. It was a sign of respect and earned trust. When people behave with respect in your presence, it not only says they respect you, it says they can trust you, too.

Trust is a vital element of life; it will determine what we get out of life. If you can be trusted, you will gain opportunities. When people trust you, they place what they value in your care. If the company trusts you, you may be appointed to a position of management. If the team trusts you, they will welcome you into a position of leadership. If we earn trust in our family, we are given decision-making responsibilities or the care of others.

While I was playing in the pros, there was a situation with a player who wanted more money. I tried to tell him that he'd get more with the success of the team. I also tried to get him to understand that he could obtain both. You have to be trusted with success before anyone just hands it to you.

Many times, we forget that trust is earned, which means we have to work toward getting it. I understood this, so I demonstrated what was necessary for me to advance in my career. It works the same way in the real world. You can't expect to have success in life and keep it, if you haven't earned it. It's better to earn it. Don't expect to have success if you are not capable of handling it. If you earn trust, people will entrust you with what they know you are capable of upholding. If trust is given to you without any trial, people will expect what you can't deliver. When it comes to trust, people will either prove you right or prove you wrong. It is best if you are honest and people are not disappointed.

In a group setting, trust becomes like the strength of a wolf pack. A team is like a pack. The strength of the entire pack is in its numbers and the way individual wolves work together as a team. A lone wolf may go hungry or need to settle for scraps or leftovers. But a pack is as strong as its members. They work as a team, and after trusting one another to do their part, they enjoy the success of the pack.

A friend of mine lives in a subdivision that backs up to almost 800 acres of woods and forest. Almost daily, my friend sees a single wolf walking across the backyards near the tree line. If you look closely, as the wolf wanders out, there are several other wolves just ten to twenty feet into the woods and brush. The "lone wolf" attracts the attention of all the family pets. If one of the pets takes off to chase the wolf, the seemingly lone wolf runs into the thick forest—where the protection and ambush of the pack awaits.

If the team is strong in one area or in executing a particular task, it can affect the performance of the team as a whole. Conversely, if the team has a weakness in an area, this could possibly threaten the achievements of the entire group. To achieve success, you must be able to trust each other that everyone will do their part. It's this systematic trust in each other that enables teams and individuals to achieve more together. In football, it means divisional titles and Super Bowl championships. In business, it's winning new big accounts and achieving company goals.

Trust is a proud possession. You should surround yourself with people you can trust and work to make sure you're operating with integrity. The foundations of trust are integrity and action. It is through these principles that trust is earned or lost. Working in a team increases accountability and builds trust and camaraderie. Even if someone doesn't share your core beliefs, you can develop a bond through teamwork. You have to reach out and give back. People want to be in your corner when they know you are a giving person.

Be a strong member of the team.

A vital component of life, trust will determine what we get out of life. If you can be trusted, you will gain opportunities. If you can't be trusted, who will present you with an opportunity?

We have to work to keep our trust. I understand that now, but I didn't always. I was fortunate that through some early disappointments and with my faith as a foundation, I learned how important trust really was. I demonstrated every Sunday night what was necessary to advance in my career, and discovered that it works the same way in the real world. You can't expect to have success in life and keep it, if you haven't earned it.

Trust is something that's earned over years or a series of interactions. When a company delivers consistently on product or service, the consumer builds trust. Look at Apple. It consistently delivers an excellent product, and the public knows what to expect. Familiarity and dependability build trust. That's why brand consistency is so important. Walk into any Apple store; it's going to look just the same as the one in your own city. The design is the same. The product is the same. There's comfort in that; you trust the product. Build a brand that delivers what you say it will and you'll build trust. Be a person who consistently honors his word and you will build trust. It's a foundation that lasts.

STEPS TO BUILD TRUST

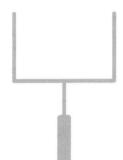

Consistency builds trust. Be consistent in truth and action.
Fulfill truths that are evident.
Do what you say you're going to do, when you say you're going to do it.

Be someone others can count on. Be consistently dependable.

STRATEGY 15

"PERSEVERANCE"

Perseverance is a trait of successful people. They've spent years striving for success, working hard, and living the principles in this book, and when things don't go their way, they just keep going. They persevere. They keep pushing as if they never had an obstacle at all.

How much strength do you have in the face of adversity? Some people seem like the cat with nine lives. They just never give up. But then others throw in the towel right away.

Have you ever known someone who never seemed to hear the word *no*? They keep on persevering.

Perseverance means to be steadfast in doing something despite difficulty. It means to continue a course of action and not be distracted by opposition or previous failures. Perseverance is required to perfect just about any skill. If you're doing something in spite of difficulty, and you're being strict on yourself, this requires perseverance. The lessons in this book are intertwined. Perseverance is linked to discipline, wisdom, integrity, and character. You need to persevere to attain major goals.

I had the benefit of learning perseverance and a lot of other great skills from my brother, Aaron, who was always a positive role model for me. He was two years older than me, so naturally as he went through experiences, I watched him. He was a great football player and athlete. He was team captain on the football team. Aaron educated me about how to behave and what I should or shouldn't do, but most of the time, I just watched him and learned from his example. Aaron was instrumental in preparing me for life. He taught me that you had to be good in sports and academics at the same time. He was highly respected by coaches, teachers, and teammates, so I had big shoes to fill. I once wanted to go to a different school because I wanted to get out of Aaron's shadow.

I grew up admiring my brother because he got a scholarship and was drafted before me. Aaron played for the Denver Broncos, and we both went in at the sixth round! If my brother hadn't been in the picture, I honestly don't know how I would have turned out. My relationship with my brother taught me the importance of a mentor. He taught me that it was good to have trustworthy people around you.

There are no short cuts to any place you're going in life.

There are a lot of kids who want to play in the NFL and the National Basketball Association, but they don't want to work at it. The journey depends on your foundation. People see the success at the end, but nobody sees the struggle and the hard work involved along the way. Getting there is hard and challenging; there were times when I wanted to give up. To be successful there are no shortcuts. Success is not free or quick, fast or easy. Success is hard work.

Who are your mentors?

In college, I was paired with another great example in my roommate, Mark Hanlon. Mark was a business student, so whenever I came back to the room after practice, he had his head in a book. Mark and I were the best of friends, and still are today. A lot of the guys were hanging out and getting caught up in distractions after practices and games. I remained disciplined enough to put time into my studies. Mark was a constant reminder for me of my responsibilities in that area. He was a good mentor and excellent role model.

A good mentor will prepare you for that journey. Some mentors are for a lifetime, and some are with you for only a short time or season in your life. In college, I also hung out with my brother and his friends who were already in the pros. Many people hang around people who make them feel good, but I wanted to hang around people better than me. There's a time to play and a time to work. I learned early in life that if you hang around knuckleheads you will do what knuckleheads do, but if you surround yourself with go-getters, they'll get you going. In the corporate world, you hang out with the people you want to be like, or the ones who are leaders. Stay away from energy-drainers and negative people.

Perseverance is like working out to get a muscle stronger, and pushing through the pain.

Perseverance is having the ability to overcome adversity, to prevail against the opposition. When we go through situations in life, we have to make choices. Sometimes we cannot and do not choose the situation we face, but we do choose how we respond to it.

Do you choose to skirt around an issue or are you determined to deal with it? If we are determined, that determination will bring forth the endurance needed to accomplish any undertaking. That's perseverance.

My son plays football. Although I've played on the professional level, I don't go to his games and try to coach him, because he has a coach. He doesn't need me to tell him what to do; he's got a path of his own. I can guide him to good character traits, strong values, and healthy disciplines, but I can't do the work for him. He's got to learn the way I did—through hard work and discipline.

I want him to learn life's lessons based on his individual efforts, work ethic, and character. He is learning the difference between having to compete and being on team. I know the situations you have to persevere through in sports. I found those experiences valuable in teaching me about life. Sports is a good teacher.

When we meet an obstacle head on and we accomplish our goals, it builds our self-esteem. When we manage to take a step forward toward persevering against the odds, we discover abilities we didn't know we had. We are able to accomplish more, and do more, when we persist in our efforts.

Athletes must persevere through injuries. I've had a bladder injury and broken bones in my foot. I had to undergo surgery for my foot, and for the first time I had to sit on the bench. It was a struggle to get back to playing football on the level I once played. People think your career is over when you get injured. However, I was blessed to overcome the injury and get back on the field. It took perseverance. When you're older and there's younger talent waiting for an opportunity to perform, it can be scary!

Situations such as this prepared me for the tougher situations that came later, such as the death of my girlfriend and my father. Not only did I have to deal with loss, but I was expected to continue to perform during my mourning. I had to carry on. I remember leaving for my father's funeral on a Friday and having to travel back for a game that Sunday.

Having to bury my father and then perform on Sunday in front of eighty thousand people was difficult. I had to compartmentalize my emotions. I had to separate them and focus my effort where it was needed the most. I had a choice to make in a moment of adversity, and so do you when unexpected obstacles appear and cloud your vision.

What happens if you have a friend or a child who isn't strong in this area? How do you teach perseverance? It's one of the most difficult things to teach because one's ability to be strong and never give up is often hidden deep inside. Jack Ma is a man who tried to interview for thirty different job opportunities. He was rejected for each one. He was even turned down by Kentucky Fried Chicken. Today, his company, Alibaba, is worth billions, and he's China's richest man. Somewhere along the way, he believed in himself enough to never give up.

Perseverance is needed in any endeavor. It says I will do what it takes to be successful. If you're in a position in life or in the company and you have to meet deadlines or make the adjustments that are necessary to complete a task, you have to be persistent to meet that goal. That means continuing the effort until the goal is completed. It's in those moments that you realize what it takes to be successful. You understand what your strengths are. Realizing you are capable of handling adversity produces confidence, and with confidence comes certainty. Being sure will almost guarantee our success; perseverance makes our goals achievable.

You not only have to work your physical muscles, you have to work your mental muscles as well. Working your mental muscles creates discipline for the routines in your life, and provides the determination to be successful. The mental focus you carry into your work routine provides you with the mental edge, or sharpness, needed to think through a plan of action. In sports, if you have to compete against an opponent who is just as talented as you, the person who's smarter is the one who will win.

In my career, I had to overcome adversity and hardship just like everyone else. Success isn't easy. It doesn't mean you are exempt from challenges. During my three stages of development—from high school, to college, and the pros—I experienced three incidents when the team I was on suffered the loss of a teammate. Incidents such as these are always horrible, but the team comes together. When you suffer the loss of a friend, you have to go on living even though a piece of you wants to crumble. If you stay stuck in the unfairness of it or the feelings surrounding it, you won't be resilient. You won't be the best you can be.

I teach my son that playing football is not the only important thing in his life, and shouldn't be his only focus because you can't play sports forever. The guy who gets cut from a team experiences the same feeling as a guy who loses his job. People who get laid off face the stress of trying to understand how they are going to provide for themselves and their families.

While I was playing professionally, I knew that I wouldn't and couldn't play football forever. There are a lot of factors involved in that.

You get older, there's younger and cheaper talent, or you may suffer an unfortunate turn of events that will not let you perform up to the level of your responsibilities or competition.

We don't get to choose our adversity, but we have the choice in how we handle it.

Many people are under the assumption that once you're drafted, you're already on a team in the pros. That's not the case. You still have to make the team once you're drafted. You also have to prepare yourself for making the team every year! Chances are, after a year or so you might get released or rejected. Players are also released due to injuries or age or lack of ability.

Imagine you were a doctor, and all of a sudden someone comes in and says, "Hey, you're too old. We are trading you in!" This doesn't happen in the medical profession like it does in sports. It does happen in the corporate world, though. In the corporate world, you can be an executive for a long time, but you must make plans for the future. Preparation and learning are always important. Contracts and jobs aren't guaranteed, and neither is success. You have to work to acquire and keep a position.

STEPS TO BUILD PERSEVERANCE

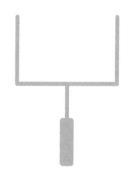

Stay committed to yourself and the knowledge that, win or lose, you're going to make it.

Be persistent in your persistence! Never give up. Great things come to those who don't.

STRATEGY 16

"SERVITUDE"

Great leaders serve others. They are servant-leaders. They lead by the example of giving.

At first glance, you might not really identify with the term *servant-leadership*. Most people believe you must be out in front to lead. They think that leadership is about knowing the way to go and using that knowledge in directing everyone else around them in what to do. But leadership is much more than that. It's not about being a dominant force that tells everyone what to do, and it's not about knowing it all.

A servant-leader leads while serving others. They place others' interests ahead of their own interests and needs. A servant-leader values the work of the team and the participation that everyone makes toward the achievement of a common goal. The servant-leader's emphasis is on the improvement of the group and the balance of power among the participants.

Servant-leaders must be good listeners. They must be sensitive to the activities of the team, and work diligently in ensuring the team and participants get the visibility and resources they need for success. They listen to their followers and value their input.

A leader who operates this way will have an abundant mindset. They are open and unafraid to share the spotlight. A leader such as this really wants to see other people win. A leader who serves will give more than anyone expects and not expect anything in return. This leader wants everyone to succeed, and gives from his abundant heart.

To understand how to serve others, you've got to be a great listener who knows what people want! How do you know unless you listen? Active listening is a communication method in which you do more than just listen. You are actively engaged and provide feedback to support the team's objectives. You've got to be a great listener who knows what people want!

Servant-leaders develop an understanding of the emotions felt by others. A servant-leader has the ability to improve themselves and others through their sense of well-being. They are generally aware of their environment and any issues that might affect their team, organization, and its members. Think of the way Herb Kelleher led Southwest Airlines. He didn't necessarily care about living up to the traditional buttoned-up airline standards, and he certainly didn't care what people thought about him. He was focused on the culture of the workplace, and how Southwest did things, honoring his employees and encouraging them. He was also focused on serving the passenger, his customer.

Inside an organization, servant-leadership means that everyone is important. Since a key trait is having everyone feel that their contributions matter, a servant-leader influences others by persuasion and reason rather than the use of authority or force. They can foresee the outcome of events or actions in which the organization is involved.

How many times have you encountered a person in a leadership position who never allowed healthy discussions in meetings? Sometimes people in leadership positions or roles in an organization feel that they must always have the say on matters, even when others may have better ideas. In these environments, over time, people attend meetings and show up on time, but they don't really participate. They may listen and maybe even take some notes, but their hearts are not anywhere near the meeting! There are many employees and athletes who go through the motions, stay under the radar, but never contribute to their maximum because of ineffective leadership.

It happens every day, even with professional athletes. I remember team sessions and meetings when some player just hogged the entire floor. They would go on a rant that had no beginning, no end, and certainly no productive points. Some players just checked out when this happened. They decided not to participate and focused on other things. As a team leader and in my servant-leader role, I had to use techniques that encouraged the team to correct itself. Using good listening skills and asking good questions encouraged people to step in and provide their perspectives. When this happened, the team prospered and we grew closer.

Chances are you're always going to have someone like I just described in any work environment. How do you handle it? You can mentor them, but you can't ridicule them. You've got to find a way to get them on the same page or get them to stop that behavior, so they don't divide the group. Servant-leadership is about gently, but firmly, leading and showing by example how to be a leader at the same time.

Have a giving mindset. Serve, and lead by example.

Servant-leaders put their vision and goals into a plan of action. When they perform duties, their objective or aim is for the betterment of the group and its members. They view their position as one of a caretaker. They assume responsibility for the group as opposed to having complete control over it. To be a servant-leader, you have to be committed to the personal growth of those who are with you.

Those who serve their communities are good examples of servant-leaders. They are committed to building mutual respect between themselves, the community, local organizations and companies. I learned that you can serve others even when you're not in your best frame of mind. Even if life isn't going your way, you can make a big contribution to the team.

I recall playing a game against the Pittsburgh Steelers, and I felt a pop in my foot. I walked off the field in pain; I knew something was wrong because I couldn't put my full weight on the foot. Once I got examined, it was confirmed that it was a break. I had been playing on artificial turf and my foot pivoted and somehow gave way to the pressure.

It was early in the game and early in the season, and I was out. I was someone who helped motivate and lead the team, and when I got hurt, I felt that I let my teammates down too. It was a big setback, but then I turned it into a setup for the future, meaning that I turned it into a positive.

When I broke my foot playing in the NFL, it was the first time I had to sit as a leader.

Someone else had to assume the leadership role on the field. I could have been the type of player who stood on the sidelines thinking only of myself. Having an understanding of what it meant to be a servant-leader, I had a greater interest in the team's success than my own. I wasn't able to lead on the field, but I was able to lead by example off the field. I was out of the game for more than two months because of the injury. Imagine having to sit on the sidelines and watch your biggest passion playing out in front of you.

This time and experience helped me later after I healed. As a result, I was a much better communicator and better at pushing teammates to higher levels of performance. I had learned that when everyone's head and hearts were engaged, the sky was the limit for our collective success.

No matter what life throws at you, there is no excuse for not being a role model or mentor. You can lead kids, adults, your family, colleagues, and especially yourself. It has to start with you.

Another example where I learned of servant-leadership was in college at the University of Utah. I had been singled out by my coaches for mistakes on the field, and as a punishment I had to run the stadium stairs from bottom to the top. It was a tradition at the university that after each game, we reviewed the game film and anyone who made a blunder had to run stairs. We called them LOEs for "lack of effort." Coaches also used LOEs as punishment for being late for a practice or a game, for not running fast enough, or if you didn't grab a fumble in a game when it could have been a game-changer. Many times, LOEs were debatable, and in this case, a few of my teammates disagreed with the coaches. But as a team leader—a servant-leader—I took the LOE and the punishment and ran the stairs. Because I was the leader, the team saw that I was dedicated to the success of the team. Sometimes being a leader means you have to display servant-leadership from whatever position you are in.

I could have complained and contested the punishment. Instead, I ran the stadium stairs. An LOE consisted of running from the bottom step of an eighty-thousand seat stadium to the very top row of seats and back. I had to do that twelve times. After my last one, I did one more—an extra! When I was done, my teammates cheered and rallied around me. I did more LOEs and stadium runs that day than anyone had the entire year. Rather than showing bad temperament in front of my teammates and coaches, I embraced the issue because I felt I would be made stronger. The harder I worked, the better I could be.

Being a servant-leader helped me understand the responsibilities of being a leader. A leader doesn't lead on his or her own terms; they recognize the needs of others and consider and appreciate the success of others. Servant-leadership is cultivating relationships within a group and looking out for the best interests of that group. It begins with choosing to serve, as opposed to being the one who wants to be served. It's a conscious choice that inspires one to lead.

STEPS TO SERVING

Leading yourself means implementing the traits in this book or similar traits that you've determined you want to live by. Develop the core values you stand for. Make a list. Which traits do you think you should work on to develop yourself as a leader? Will you vow to live by and serve from them? It takes this kind of dedication to be a true servant-leader. To whom will you give back? Plan now, and leave a legacy.

STRATEGY 17

"ADAPTABILITY"

Curveballs come in life. You may expect one play, but the opponent does something different. Life throws things you don't expect.

High achievers are adaptable. How adaptable are you? This might be an area in which you'll want to assess yourself. Are you as flexible as you need to be? Do you tend to stay stuck in problems after you've hit an obstacle? You have to be adaptable enough to respond effectively and swiftly to change. When something happens that's out of your control, respond with grace and adapt. Don't be the one to protest, whine, or hang onto the past. You can certainly protest real injustices; I'm not talking about that. Adaptability means you'll be ready for anything at any time. And age isn't an excuse! You've heard the phrase, "You can't teach old dogs new tricks," but that's just not true. Sometimes it's the younger ones who are more firm and arrogant in their ways. It's not about age. It's about being adaptable to a variety of situations and embracing change.

London marathon runner Fauja Singh was nominated for a British Empire Medal by the Queen of England for his services to sport and charity. That's a remarkable designation. But what's even more remarkable is that he's 103 years old! He became the world's oldest marathon runner by being extremely adaptable and taking the challenge head on. He started his running career at 89 and ended up in international marathon events.

It's reported that he thought that a marathon was just twenty-six kilometers, and that he could achieve it. When he learned it was twenty-six miles instead, he didn't get intimidated or quit. He continued to train and got even more disciplined about training seriously. The challenge was the fuel to inspire him to train more seriously. Talk about adaptability!

Mr. Singh, who was born in 1911, took up running in his 80s to distract himself from the trauma of losing his son, daughter, and wife. All that loss could have crippled him, but instead he found a way to adapt. Speaking about the marathon, he said: "The first twenty miles are not difficult. As for last six miles, I run while talking to God."

I share this story because I hope it inspires you as much as it did me. There's always a chance to adapt to make things better, to give back, or to overcome. You have the choice to adapt or to remain where you are. Sometimes where you are isn't good and it's time to change. Other times you're perfectly comfortable, and change just happens. If you're at work, for instance, and the boss you love gets fired, you can either choose to view it as a great injustice and become bitter, angry, or rebellious; or you can roll with the changes and adapt to the new boss. Each one of these situations requires a choice. It's up to you.

Life is never without confusion, change, or unexpected events and surprises. They're not always good, but they can be turned to the good if you've got the right attitude. Make a commitment to be adaptable and impossible to offend.

My job as captain of the defense was to make adjustments. The free safety and I made the necessary audibles and last second defensive play changes during the game. Usually, both of us were on the same page, but if there was any confusion, my decisions had more weight. Doing this took a lot of preparation during film time; we also needed to be on the same page with the coaches. I was a quiet leader. But to be effective, I also had to be an effective player in my position. I had to earn it.

Employers are looking for potential employees who have strong adaptability. In fact, adaptability is ranked as one of the highest work attributes along with communication, interpersonal skills, and a strong work ethic. Every company structure, workplace atmosphere, and culture is different. Every company, every team, looks for a candidate who fits within the existing work environment and is able to anticipate, respond to, and manage change on a day-to-day basis.

Each organization has its own workplace subculture that is strategically important for the company's success. When hiring, companies consider not only a candidate's experience and skills, but also how that potential employee will mesh with their company's culture.

Adaptability is even more important when you rise through the ranks and become a manager or leader within a larger company. The impact you have on the culture and employees depends on your adaptability, as others watch how you respond to the ever-changing marketplace.

In business as well as sports, your ideas are not always well accepted. To fit in and be a productive player or teammate, you may have to adapt to another idea, plan, or strategy—one you may not totally like or support.

When you understand what character traits you stand for, adaptability will come more naturally. If you decide to be adaptable, you will be.

I always tried to play for something greater than myself. My spir-

> **Be adaptable! It makes life easier.**

ituality and playing for God was important to me. He had given me some natural gifts and abilities and provided me this opportunity in the NFL, and I did not want to let him down.

Some fellow team members couldn't adapt to being celebrities, and fame's subsequent need for time management and commitment. They played for a short time or were relegated to practice squads and never made it to the level to which their potential pointed. When you can't focus, you lose a lot.

I knew that I was given a small window to maximize a blessing. Why get caught up in distractions such as alcohol, drugs, and women. These temptations were always around and available, and I was determined that they would not sidetrack me.

Success and celebrity status only make you more of what you are. If you are a womanizer or lazy to begin with, being a celebrity will make you more of a womanizer and lazier. I was by no means perfect, but I was determined and I worked hard to stay focused on this blessing I had been given.

There are sacrifices that you have to make. You have to sacrifice things to be the best. Kobe Bryant has played since age eighteen as one of the most prolific players in the NBA. But he had to separate himself from many of his friends. He developed his "Black Mamba" persona to survive. On the field, I was called the "Silent Assassin." I wasn't always the most vocal guy, so when I said something, it was important. On the field, I let my actions do the talking, and my teammates and opponents respected me for it. Off the field, I was a good guy and I separated the two personas.

Not being able to turn it off sometimes causes problems, especially when you transition your on-the-field persona to your relationships. Some people can't separate the two, and when this happens, trouble is not far behind. You've got to be the family man at home and the athletic monster on the field!

When I played, I was one of 32 linebackers in the entire NFL. It was a blessing and I worked hard to honor that position. But off the field, I was just another citizen.

People who are not adaptable tend to be stressed all the time.

People who are not adaptable tend to be stressed all the time. They let situations and lofty expectations seep into their daily life and actions. How many of your colleagues are always complaining about things they cannot control? They always seem worked up about something. One thing is a constant, and that is change. When you work in a company, change is everywhere, every day. Whether it's a new process, reorganization, or change in markets, you will be asked to accommodate change.

Sometimes life's unexpected changes can cause stress, but at other times, stress is self-imposed because we haven't planned well enough. For instance, an NFL player who makes millions during his career has to be wise. He's not always going to make millions. This is where planned adaptability comes into play. Have you planned for the future? I've seen a lot of football players who have not. It's not just a financial adaptation for which you've got to prepare, but an emotional transition and a physical one, too. Studies of centenarians show that the ones who are healthy and live to that age have a high adaptability rate. They've been able to make transitions from driving to not driving; from being in control to relying on others; and to intentionally become more social. They've adapted physically and emotionally, too.

Adaptability is important in all areas of your life. It's easier to adapt if you think ahead and plan for future changes. When you're eighty, chances are you won't have the same physical mobility you had your entire life. You've got to plan for where you'll live, what you'll do, how you'll get around, and who you'll be with, as much as you can. Imagine the person who hasn't thought about any of this. Imagine the athlete, executive, or individual worker who hasn't planned for their financial future, or the spouse who hasn't prepared for the changes their husband or wife might want to make. Imagine the mother whose only child is leaving for college. If she hasn't prepared for it emotionally, it could be devastating. Imagine the CEO who retires and doesn't fly around in the corporate jet anymore or get picked up in the limo. He can't expect to have the same perks he used to have. He worked hard for that position, and even if he has the income, the emotional transition can be difficult.

When Tiki Barber, the retired New York Giants running back, was interviewed about his transition from sports, he said that it was very difficult. He said he watched so many movies and television episodes that he was in a slump at thirty-five. He was depressed. When you reach that state, you might feel as if you've been replaced. Your glory days are gone. Someone younger and better has replaced you. But that's not true! You've got to keep on going and find more joy in life; you've got to be adaptable enough to try new things and find a different career or passion you can focus on.

People who aren't adaptable tend be uncomfortable when faced with new, unexpected, and urgent projects. This negative approach works its way into their performance; they think others perceive them in an unfavorable light. This translates into more stress and pressure to perform. To show that you're a team player, and that you're flexible and adaptable, you need to be willing to take on tasks or projects when urgency and change are key. When you have the ability to remain calm and are considered adaptable, your work will improve and the organization will consider you more valuable.

In most organizations, adaptability must be demonstrated every day for someone to be considered for a leadership position. To adapt and stay calm to the challenges a company will face is especially important for organizational leaders. It's the leadership team that will set the tone for employees. Adaptable leaders and flexible employees are the ones who show a balance of calm and quick reaction, and usually pass on those traits to others. They are important assets of the organization.

STEPS TO BECOME MORE ADAPTABLE

Don't think of a loss or failure as the end of the world. When things don't go your way, find another way.

Be open to change. Start looking at changes as exciting opportunities instead of something scary.

Plan to be the most flexible, adaptable person in the world in order to strengthen your relationships.

As a leader of a household, company, or team, you've got to be able to handle curveballs when things don't go your way.

Ask your mentor to help you assess your adaptability.

STRATEGY 18

"CHOICE"

There's one thing that each one of these rules has in common, and that's the ability to choose whether or not to live by them. At the end of the day, it's up to you. Your choices make up who you are and what you'll do in this world. Are you choosing the right things? Are you taking responsibility for your successes and failures? When you choose the right things, the path is much easier. When you choose the wrong things, the path is difficult and complex, and there are a whole lot more roadblocks.

As great a golfer as Tiger Woods is, some of his choices led to a very public disruption in his career, as well as the loss of his marriage. All, caused by choices. Did his successes go to his head or ruin him?

I don't think you can blame everything on success or privilege. It doesn't matter if you're rich or poor. We all have the same opportunity to make good choices. Tiger is one of the best golfers in the world and has been applauded for bringing diversity to the sport. But in my opinion his legacy was tarnished. The stories that came out about him portrayed him in a much different light than the disciplined, wholesome, family man reputation he had built. What if he hadn't had that blemish on his legacy?

Most of us have had imperfect pasts and have made mistakes, but when I see others making mistakes, it's a reminder to me that the choice is mine. There's power in choice. You have one body, and you can choose to be healthy and eat right and exercise—or not. You have one mind, and you can fill it with junk or watch what you read, listen to, or think about. You have one soul, too, and you can nourish it or expose yourself to all kinds of garbage.

Make the right choice.

The world will always offer you garbage, whether it's sex, drugs, an illicit affair, the chance to lie or cheat for gain, or to take the easy shortcut. Even if a decision is not something obviously unethical, it might not lead to good things. Short-term gain isn't always the best choice. Weigh your decisions carefully.

What happens when you've made bad choices?

No one is perfect. No one goes through their entire life without making mistakes. I've made plenty, and you will, too. Our parents and grandparents made mistakes! The decision to make the best choice in light of them is what's important. Once you've made a mistake and discovered it, your next step and the choices you make will determine your future.

Often our choices have a domino effect that impacts everyone around us. If someone makes a decision to drink and drive, it can lead to a tragedy on the road; it can impact a totally different family. If someone makes a choice to lash out and fight in anger, it can lead to the destruction of a career. Emotions cannot be the barometer for making your choices. Feelings are not trustworthy guideposts—character traits and values are.

Personally, I make my choices from a foundation of faith.

I know that if I'm angry or frustrated, I can always pause and stop to think about what choice I'm going to make. When I work with youth who are facing a big and uncertain world, I want to explain to them the importance of thinking ahead, and not acting out or reacting to others. People will try to intimidate you, taunt you, or get you to react in a negative way. Will you respond out of anger? Will you lose your career over a fight? Will you manage your stress with alcohol, drugs, promiscuity, or worldly things that can threaten your family and career? I coach young men to stay focused on their dream, and delete the distractions. There's no dream that comes with toxic things that hurt your mind or body. Your legacy is worth much more than that.

STEPS TO MAKE THE RIGHT CHOICES

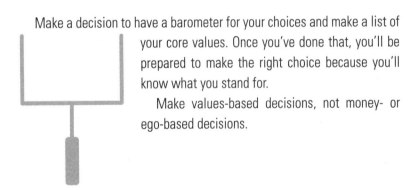

Make a decision to have a barometer for your choices and make a list of your core values. Once you've done that, you'll be prepared to make the right choice because you'll know what you stand for.

Make values-based decisions, not money- or ego-based decisions.

Focus on making the right choice at the right time, all the time.

HARD WORK AND DISCIPLINE LEAD TO STRENGTH AND PERSEVERANCE THAT CANNOT BE REPLACED.

- Visit alsmithallpro.com
- Be a mentor to someone who needs one.
- Invite Al Smith to speak at your event.
- Get involved in your community.
- Share the strategies in this book.

It Only Takes One

Be adaptable! It makes life easier.

If you're a fan of this book, Please tell others...

- Write about *Think Like A Pro – Act Like A Pro* on your blog, Facebook and Twitter.

- Suggest the book to your friends, co-workers, neighbors and family.

- When you're in a bookstore, ask them if they carry the book. This book is available through all major distributors, any bookstore that does not have this book can easily stock it!

- Write a positive review of *Think Like A Pro – Act Like A Pro* on www.amazon.com

- Purchase additional copies to give away as gifts.

- Connect at: alsmithallpro.com

To order another copy write us at HigherLife Publishing and Marketing PO Box 623307 Oviedo, FL 32762 or email us info@ahigherlife.com.